A BRIEF COMMENTARY
ON THE
ACTS OF THE APOSTLES

by
John J. Kilgallen, S.J.

PAULIST PRESS
New York/Mahwah

Library of Congress Cataloging-in-Publication Data

Kilgallen, John J.
    A brief commentary on the Acts of the Apostles / by John J. Kilgallen.
      p.   cm.
    ISBN 0-8091-2977-9 (pbk.) :
      1. Bible. N.T. Acts—Commentaries.   I. Title.
BS2625.3.K55   1988
226'.607—dc19   88-2324
                                                                    CIP

Published by Paulist Press
997 Macarthur Blvd.
Mahwah, N.J. 07430

Printed and bound in the United States of America

Contents

iii

Introduction

In the Introduction to my first volume, concerning the Gospel of Luke, I laid emphasis on the vision of Luke which included both the life of Jesus in Palestine and the subsequent events in which the offer of salvation in his name spread throughout the Mediterranean Basin. My first volume coincided with Luke's Gospel, tracing the development of Jesus' life out of the Old Testament, through teaching and healing in Galilee and through a journey to the right hand of God which involved death and resurrection. In Jesus' life-story, Luke presented us with a number of perceptions of the identity of Jesus: even his pre-conception and infancy stories, which serve as introduction to the adult Jesus, revealed Jesus to be, in particular, Son of God, Lord, Messiah and a light to all the nations. Jesus, we learn from his baptism to his ascension, was a forgiver of sins, a healer and wonder-worker, a teacher for human happiness in relation to God and to human beings, a just prophet unjustly killed, a glorious fulfillment of Jewish Scriptures which talked about the Messiah as one who "had" to die and "had" to rise.

Certain aspects of the Gospel were clearly intended to be fulfilled only after Jesus' death and resurrection, e.g., his enlightenment of the nations, the founding of a particular group to be fishers of men, the teachings about what discipleship would mean when Jesus was absent. Most partic-

1

ularly, though the Gospel presents an ending in which Jesus gloriously returns to his Father amidst the joy of his disciples, it also asks that the disciples "wait in Jerusalem to be clothed in power." This empowerment of the Holy Spirit makes the Gospel reader look beyond the life of Jesus to the witnessing to his saving name. Luke insists that the Jewish Scriptures saw this time of witnessing as necessary as the life of the Messiah himself. Luke, then, asks his Gospel reader to turn to the continuation of the mission of Jesus, the Savior, a mission directed by him from his Father's right hand and reaching all men and women of every place and every time—even to Theophilus. From what Theophilus has read in the Gospel and from what he will read in the Acts, he and others like him will realize how firm and reliable are the truths which they have been taught. They will see themselves as the logical and correct recipients of what had been foretold in the Jewish Scriptures, begun by Jesus in Palestine and faithfully, truthfully carried to them by authorized witnesses of the Lord Jesus. Let us now look to this extension of the Lord's work beyond his Palestinian life, as his becomes the name the Scriptures had foretold, upon which one—anyone—calls for salvation. For his is the only name given to men on earth by which one can be saved.

Preparations for Pentecost: Jesus Teaches, Departs • Matthias Replaces Judas

With the immediate mention of "my former work," "Theophilus," and the temporal framework "from the beginning to the being taken up," Luke begins Acts with the recollection of the Gospel. The Gospel and Acts are thus intimately parts of a whole, complementing each other, making fuller sense of each other. In particular, Luke summarizes his earlier work as a presentation of Jesus' words and deeds; in this way he is asking his reader to pay close attention to elements which the disciples will soon be in a position to give witness to, for what Jesus did and said are being remembered for the benefit of the reader, for the benefit of Luke's contemporaries who have committed their lives to the Lord of these words and deeds and will now appreciate being told how these words and deeds, written up with such fervor and care and insight in the Gospel, found their way unadulterated to themselves. We are to follow the witnesses to these words and deeds.

One might have assumed it, but Luke makes clear now what he did not mention expressly at the time in his Gospel narrative: the apostles (= "sent out") were chosen through the direction of the Holy Spirit, the very Spirit involved in the creation of Jesus and in guiding him to begin his mission as anointed by the Spirit (Lk 4:18–19). The same force now is recognized as influential in the witnesses to Jesus.

Luke's note that Jesus appeared many times to the apostles over a period of forty days must be understood against

1 In the first book, O Theophilus, I have dealt with all that Jesus began to do and teach, ²until the day when he was taken up, after he had given commandment through the Holy Spirit to the apostles whom he had chosen. ³To them he presented himself alive after his passion by many proofs, appearing to them during forty days, and speaking of the kingdom of God. ⁴And while staying with them he charged them not to depart from Jerusalem, but to wait for the promise of the Father, which, he said, "you heard from me, ⁵for John baptized with water, but before many days you shall be baptized with the Holy Spirit."

6 So when they had come together, they asked him, "Lord, will you at this time restore the kingdom to Israel?" ⁷He said to them, "It is not for you to know times or seasons which the Father has fixed by his own authority. ⁸But you shall receive power when the Holy Spirit has come upon you; and you shall be my witnesses in Jerusalem and in all Judea and Samaria and to the end of the earth." ⁹And when he had said this, as they were looking on, he was lifted up, and a cloud took him out of their sight. ¹⁰And while they were gazing into heaven as he went, behold, two men stood by them in white robes, ¹¹and said, "Men of Galilee, why do you stand looking into heaven? This Jesus, who was taken up from you into heaven, will come in the same way as you saw him go into heaven."

12 Then they returned to Jerusalem from the mount called Olivet, which is near Jerusalem, a sabbath day's journey away; ¹³and when they had entered, they

went up to the upper room, where they were staying, Peter and John and James and Andrew, Philip and Thomas, Bartholomew and Matthew, James the son of Alphaeus and Simon the Zealot and Judas the son of James. [14]All these with one accord devoted themselves to prayer, together with the women and Mary the mother of Jesus, and with his brothers.

15 In those days Peter stood up among the brethren (the company of persons was in all about a hundred and twenty), and said, [16]"Brethren, the scripture had to be fulfilled, which the Holy Spirit spoke beforehand by the mouth of David, concerning Judas who was guide to those who arrested Jesus. [17]For he was numbered among us, and was allotted his share in this ministry. [18](Now this man bought a field with the reward of his wickedness; and falling headlong he burst open in the middle and all his bowels gushed out. [19]And it became known to all the inhabitants of Jerusalem, so that the field was called in their language Akeldama, that is, Field of Blood.) [20]For it is written in the book of Psalms,

'Let his habitation become desolate,
and let there be no one to live in it';
and
'His office let another take.'

[21]So one of the men who have accompanied us during all the time that the Lord Jesus went in and out among us, [22]beginning from the baptism of John until the day when he was taken up from us—one of these men must become with us a witness to his resurrection." [23]And they put forward two, Joseph called Barsabbas, who was surnamed Justus, and Matthias. [24]And they prayed and said, "Lord, who knowest the hearts of all men, show which one of these two thou hast chosen [25]to take the place in this ministry and apostleship from which Judas turned

aside, to go to his own place." [26]And they cast lots for them, and the lot fell on Matthias; and he was enrolled with the eleven apostles.

the sure conclusion that, if Jesus was raised to life, he was raised immediately to the right hand of his Father; we cannot assume that Jesus, risen, delayed his union with his Father for forty days. Thus, it is the Jesus who is at the right hand of his Father who occasionally shows himself to his apostles—and it is to teach them further about the kingdom of God and to convince them absolutely that he is risen.

That Jesus continues his teaching about the kingdom shows that his death was only a momentary halt to his main work as teacher; it probably also means that certain understandings about the kingdom come clear, once one realizes that Jesus is risen. That Jesus goes out of his way to make sure his disciples know him to be risen is motivated by the fact that Jesus risen means that Jesus was always innocent and should not have been condemned (but rather believed in), that Jesus is the beloved of God, that he is reinstated as the one and only Savior of human beings. The resurrection, in other words, means "business as usual," as it was before the sad events of the last Passover in Jerusalem.

Luke includes in these forty days of meetings a reference to the imminent descent of the Holy Spirit, a reference similar to that Luke made at the end of the Gospel. Again, Jesus presents the Spirit as the fulfillment of the Father; with such a reference Luke continues to pursue his goal of showing how the present era is the dynamic completion of the law and the prophets. In this presentation the coming of the Spirit is described as a baptism (= "immersion"); earlier it had been described as a "clothing in power" (Lk 24:49). John's baptism had signified cleansing; baptism in the Spirit means the gift of God's Holy Spirit as a consequence of the love of God which forgives.

Luke now moves to the last of the elements he wants his readers to hear before Acts begins properly with Pentecost. The disciples, like so many other Jews, had received

Jesus within their hope that God would give them entry into the kingdom of God. There were many aspects to this kingdom: wisdom, power, goodness, prosperity, adoration of the one and only God. One characteristic of the kingdom, drawn from the Old Testament, was that Israel, God's beloved, would be glorified as it takes the place among nations owed to the beloved of God; implicit in this, of course, is freedom from all enemies, including Rome, and the right to condemn, in the final judgment, those who have afflicted Israel. Now, if Jesus has been judged to be the one God designated to begin this "new age," he surely cannot leave without bringing the kingdom in its fullness into being; if he does not do it now, then when?

Luke's readers stood far enough away from the time of Jesus (we calculate about fifty to sixty years) to doubt very seriously that the kingdom of God was "at hand," that is, simultaneous with the Life of Jesus in Galilee or within a few years of that life. One can no longer say with confidence that the coming of the kingdom coincides with the lifetime of Jesus, even roughly; one even begins to wonder if Jesus' intimate relationship with God should be described with the term " Messiah."

In anticipation of these questions, Luke tells the answer to the question, "Now are you going to restore the kingdom to Israel?" Jesus' remarks are twofold. First, the kingdom will come, but the time or occasion is in the Father's mind and is not to be revealed; thus, one is to live one's life without expectation that the moment is "at hand," though in fact it might just be at hand. Second, since one is no longer preoccupied with immediate or imminent change of the ages, one should be preoccupied with something else: the disciples are to be witnesses from Jesus and about Jesus, starting in Jerusalem (Acts 2—7), moving through Judaea and Samaria (Acts 8—12), and traveling to the ends of the earth (Acts

13–28). Indeed, this role of witnesses is the central activity of Acts; all else, and whatever else Church might mean, is included in Acts only in relation to witnessing to Jesus. For better or for worse, it is for this reason that we do not have a clearer understanding of the Church in these decades; Luke subordinates all else to the activity of witnessing.

Jesus has explained the role which is central to Luke's second volume: Jesus alive is to be continued as live to all people. His being lifted up now to his Father indicates only that the special appearances of Jesus over forty days are ended; it does not mean that Jesus is no longer active as Savior—quite the contrary, as we will see. The apostles are given the assurance not simply that Jesus will return, but that his next coming to them will be in power. It will be that day of the Son of Man (Lk 21:27–28) which brings to the faithful the fullness of salvation.

The disciples return to Jerusalem, only about a walk of a thousand yards (Jews were not allowed to walk further on the sabbath, for to walk further implied that one was "working" on the sabbath). Presumably, the upper room where they stay is the upper room of the Last Supper. Luke gives again the list of the Eleven (John is now second in this listing, for he will play a significant role soon in Acts); the total number in the upper room is one hundred and twenty— the women, Mary and relatives of Jesus among them. They are pictured, for the first of many times, as persevering in prayer, presumably a form of contact with Jesus as well as with God, his Father.

To give the fullest meaning to Pentecost, the full number of the Twelve must be re-established. To this end, Luke now relates God's selection of Matthias to replace Judas. Just as Judas' fate was foretold in the Old Testament, that he would buy a field with blood money and thus no one would live in it, so the same Old Testament indicates that "someone should take his office." The necessity that Scripture be fulfilled is what moves things along; what God has said must come true.

As far as the disciples have a part in the selection of a successor for Judas (whose traitor's death is described a bit differently by Matthew—27:3–10), they note criteria which enhance the notion Luke insists upon: (eye-)witness. One must have been with us from the baptism of John to the ascension; one is particularly to be able to witness the resurrection. With these criteria brought to the attention of the reader, and within a context of prayer, God makes his selection—and we are ready to begin the volume of witnessing, with Pentecost.

2

Pentecost and Peter's Explanation of It • The Effects of Pentecost

Luke has described the eventual gift of the Spirit as a being clothed in power and as a baptism or immersion. Now he links the outpouring of the Spirit with Pentecost; why might he have done this?

Pentecost (− "fifty days") is the name of a Jewish feast which occurs fifty days after the feast of Unleavened Bread and the feast of Passover. As the feast of Unleavened Bread started off the springtime harvest, so the feast of Pentecost celebrated the end of the harvest of God's blessings. Also, it can be said that, as Passover celebrated the departure of Israel from Egypt to go to its God and the promised land, so Pentecost recalls the arrival of Israel, fifty days away from Egypt, at Mount Sinai where, with the reception of the law, Israel formalized the agreement or covenant with God which made Israel "God's people," and Yahweh "Israel's God." Scholars suggest that either or both of these meanings of Pentecost are likely to be applied to the Christian event occurring at the time of the Jewish feast of Pentecost: the outpouring of the Spirit is a completion of Jesus' death and resurrection fifty days earlier; the outpouring of the Spirit is the formal moment when God creates his community of worshipers "in the Spirit." Indeed, in relation to this latter significance, the sound of a great wind, the shaking of the house, and the flames suggest to many that Luke uses these details to make us think of the fearsome natural phenomena associated with Sinai.

2 When the day of Pentecost had come, they were all together in one place. ²And suddenly a sound came from heaven like the rush of a mighty wind, and it filled all the house where they were sitting. ³And there appeared to them tongues as of fire, distributed and resting on each one of them. ⁴And they were all filled with the Holy Spirit and began to speak in other tongues, as the Spirit gave them utterance.

5 Now there were dwelling in Jerusalem Jews, devout men from every nation under heaven. ⁶And at this sound the multitude came together, and they were bewildered, because each one heard them speaking in his own language. ⁷And they were amazed and wondered, saying, "Are not all these who are speaking Galileans? ⁸And how is it that we hear, each of us in his own native language? ⁹Parthians and Medes and Elamites and residents of Mesopotamia, Judea and Cappadocia, Pontus and Asia, ¹⁰Phrygia and Pamphylia, Egypt and the parts of Libya belonging to Cyrene, and visitors from Rome, both Jews and proselytes, ¹¹Cretans and Arabians, we hear them telling in our own tongues the mighty works of God." ¹²And all were amazed and perplexed, saying to one another, "What does this mean?" ¹³But others mocking said, "They are filled with new wine."

14 But Peter, standing with the eleven, lifted up his voice and addressed them, "Men of Judea and all who dwell in Jerusalem, let this be known to you, and give ear to my words. ¹⁵For these men are not drunk, as you suppose, since it is only the third hour of the day; ¹⁶but this is what was spoken by the prophet Joel:

[17]"And in the last days it shall be, God declares,
   that I will pour out my Spirit upon all flesh,
   and your sons and your daughters shall prophesy,
   and your young men shall see visions,
   and your old men shall dream dreams;
[18]yea, and on my menservants and my
        maidservants in those days
   I will pour out my Spirit; and they shall
        prophesy.
[19]And I will show wonders in the heaven above
   and signs on the earth beneath,
   blood, and fire, and vapor of smoke;
[20]the sun shall be turned into darkness
   and the moon into blood,
   before the day of the Lord comes,
   the great and manifest day.
[21]And it shall be that whoever calls on the name of
        the Lord shall be saved.'

22 "Men of Israel, hear these words: Jesus of Nazareth, a man attested to you by God with mighty works and wonders and signs which God did through him in your midst, as you yourselves know— [23]this Jesus, delivered up according to the definite plan and foreknowledge of God, you crucified and killed by the hands of lawless men. [24]But God raised him up, having loosed the pangs of death, because it was not possible for him to be held by it. [25]For David says concerning him,
   'I saw the Lord always before me,
      for he is at my right hand that I may not be
         shaken;
[26]therefore my heart was glad, and my tongue
      rejoiced;
   moreover my flesh will dwell in hope.
[27]For thou wilt not abandon my soul to Hades,

nor let thy Holy One see corruption.
[28]Thou hast made known to me the ways of life;
thou wilt make me full of gladness with thy
presence.'

29 "Brethren, I may say to you confidently of the patriarch David that he both died and was buried, and his tomb is with us to this day. [30]Being therefore a prophet, and knowing that God had sworn with an oath to him that he would set one of his descendants upon his throne, [31]he foresaw and spoke of the resurrection of the Christ, that he was not abandoned to Hades, nor did his flesh see corruption. [32]This Jesus God raised up, and of that we all are witnesses. [33]Being therefore exalted at the right hand of God, and having received from the Father the promise of the Holy Spirit, he has poured out this which you see and hear. [34]For David did not ascend into the heavens; but he himself says,

'The Lord said to my Lord, Sit at my right hand,
[35]till I make thy enemies a stool for thy feet.'
[36]Let all the house of Israel therefore know assuredly that God has made him both Lord and Christ, this Jesus whom you crucified."

37 Now when they heard this they were cut to the heart, and said to Peter and the rest of the apostles, "Brethren, what shall we do?" [38]And Peter said to them, "Repent, and be baptized every one of you in the name of Jesus Christ for the forgiveness of your sins; and you shall receive the gift of the Holy Spirit. [39]For the promise is to you and to your children and to all that are far off, every one whom the Lord our God calls to him." [40]And he testified with many other words and exhorted them, saying, "Save yourselves from this crooked generation." [41]So those who received his word were baptized, and there were added that day about three thousand souls.

⁴²And they devoted themselves to the apostles' teaching and fellowship, to the breaking of bread and the prayers.

43 And fear came upon every soul; and many wonders and signs were done through the apostles. ⁴⁴And all who believed were together and had all things in common; ⁴⁵and they sold their possessions and goods and distributed them to all, as any had need. ⁴⁶And day by day, attending the temple together and breaking bread in their homes, they partook of food with glad and generous hearts, ⁴⁷praising God and having favor with all the people. And the Lord added to their number day by day those who were being saved.

Luke's full treatment of Pentecost, however, leads us to another realization, that the outpouring of the Spirit upon the one hundred and twenty Christians in the upper room leads directly to speaking of the wonderful things of God. Pentecost results in prophecy ("pro" = "on behalf of"; "phecy" = "to speak"; hence, "prophecy" really means "to speak on behalf of God"). With this understanding of Pentecost as that gift which enables one to speak on behalf of God, one can understand why Jesus earlier had referred to it as a "clothing in *power*," why fire is presented as *tongues* (remember that Isaiah's lips were cleansed by fire so that he could speak on behalf of God), why the disciples had to undergo Pentecost before they began their role as witnesses—they had to be immersed in the Spirit in order to witness on behalf of God and Jesus. To Catholics, this Pentecostal baptism seems more like present-day confirmation, the sacrament of strength for witnessing.

Indeed, the complete description of Pentecost focuses on the ability of the disciples to witness to all Israelites, thus underlining witness to God as an ever more universal witness; we already know that the witness to Jesus will reach "the ends of the earth." Thus, the disciples' ability to be understood in the languages of the then-known world, the recitation of the list of nations to whom the disciples speak in miniature—this all goes to suggest that with this outpouring of the Spirit the disciples are empowered to do all that will be narrated in the rest of Acts; thus, this is not just one outpouring or empowering of the disciples, but the reason for all other, future interventions of the Spirit. The Spirit is now alive in the Church.

Peter's speech gives still another understanding of the meaning of this outpouring of the Spirit; to understand the speech we must pay attention to certain pre-suppositions, first. The fullness of Messiahship is the Messiah's actually ruling over the kingdom of God; for Luke, Jesus exercises, as the Gospel has shown, certain of the characteristics of the Messiah and thus is Messiah, but will only exercise the fullness of the Messianic role when he rules fully. Prior to this complete rule (note how we are talking of a *royal* Messiah, that one who is to rule forever over Israel as successor to David), we should expect that the Messiah will take his throne, which is at the right hand of the Father. To reach the right hand of the Father, however, implies that the Father will take the Messiah to himself someday (= the ascension). Now, in the case of Jesus, who *had* to die, God had first to raise Jesus from death, then bring him to himself, for only a live person could be Messiah. A final presupposition: though the terms "Messiah" and "Lord" need not mean the same thing, they can be interchanged if one understands Messiah to be a kingly ruler and Lord to be a kingly ruler— as happens often in the Old Testament and is presupposed often by Luke. These, then, are the presuppositions; let us look at Peter's speech, which depends on them.

The initial effort of Peter is to establish that the cause of the speech on behalf of God which his audience has just heard and acknowledged as wonderful is God's Spirit. His argument is simple. Joel, about 360 B.C., had said that someday God would pour out his Spirit; the result of this would be prophecy, speaking on behalf of God. Now we have actual speaking on behalf of God, actual prophecy; should we not argue backward, that this speaking on behalf of God is an effect, the cause of which is the Spirit of God? After all, God did say this would happen someday. But to have concluded that the Spirit has been poured out is only the beginning of Peter's argument; the main point he wants to make is still to come.

Note that Luke quotes more of the Joel prophecy than is necessary to prove that the Spirit is the cause of the disciples' speaking in prophecy; following upon prophecy, the quotation from Joel continues, will be signs and wonders, fearsome natural phenomena, the arrival of the day of judgment, and, when the Lord comes on his day to judge, those who are still faithful to him will be saved by calling on his name. Why does Luke quote so much of Joel's prophecy? Because he wants to show that with the outpouring of the Spirit the reader of Acts is in these last days! Jesus has already worked signs and wonders, but now his disciples will work them. We are getting ever closer to that day of the Lord, upon whose name we should call for salvation.

But there is an added feature in this scheme of the last days begun with the outpouring of the Spirit. If one will call now on the name of the Lord (i.e., commit himself to the Lord), then, when the day of the Lord comes, he can call on the Lord's name with confidence and enjoy the fullness of salvation which he had begun to enjoy when he first called on the name of the Lord. In short, for Luke, the outpouring of the Spirit means that *now* God is willing to save those who call upon the Lord's name, with a view to the fullest salvation on the Lord's day.

One more matter must be clarified before Peter stops speaking: What is the Lord's name? For Joel it was Yahweh; for Luke, however, it is Jesus. To show this to his audience, Peter briefly rehearses that part of Jesus' life which they had experienced, the part which already showed him to be Messiah. Peter then spends time on that part of Jesus' life which his audience has not experienced: despite what they did to Jesus, Jesus rose from the dead, ascended to God's right hand, and after pouring out the Spirit of this day, sits on his throne at the Father's right hand. To sit on that throne, Peter argues, is to merit the title "Lord," as David himself says. To be raised from the dead is to be the anointed successor of David, as David had long ago said. Jesus has been raised from the dead, has been taken to heaven, sits at the Father's right hand. This royal Messiah is, then, Lord. It is on his name that one should now call for salvation.

In light of Peter's interpretation of Pentecost, therefore, we can conclude that, for Luke, Pentecost means that *now* one can be saved by calling on the Lord's name, and that the Lord's name to call upon is Jesus. It is not surprising, then, that Peter urges his audience to repent of their sins (the consistent teaching of Jesus in the Gospel) with a view to their forgiveness, to be baptized into Jesus (= to commit one's life to Jesus as one's Lord) and to receive the Spirit of God which God had promised would one day belong to those who become his dearest. To be saved is to be saved from those who have committed themselves to find their happiness in this age and apart from God.

The speech of Peter is of immense value as the opening speech of Acts; the beliefs it contains justify the entire rest of the book and explain it. What moves the audience of the speech to accept Jesus as Lord is not only Peter's speech, but his subsequent brief encouragements and what Luke describes as the "many arguments" Peter went on to give "over a long period of time." We do not know what those arguments were, but his speech does give us some very clear hints of them; throughout Acts, Christians and Jews will spend long days and weeks and months on what was to them the basic argument: Does Jesus, in all his particulars, square with words God had spoken through the Sacred Scripture?

Luke can conclude his treatment of Pentecost only after he has described the life of the believers, for it is this life committed to Jesus which completes the outpouring of the Spirit. This life is characterized as a life faithful to the teaching of the apostles; these apostles are those eye-witnesses whose credibility Luke has worked so hard to establish and who witness not only to Jesus' teaching, but to his deeds

and his life. This life is also characterized by a concrete
expression of what Jesus had identified as the two greatest
desires of God: love of God and love of neighbor. Given the
circumstances of the moment, the judgment as to how to
love one's neighbor was to live together and share in common; given the circumstances of the moment, the way to
love God was to worship him in the sacrifices and prayers
of Judaism and to celebrate the Eucharist, as Jesus had asked.
Those Jews who watched them were greatly impressed—
impressed too by the signs and wonders worked by the
apostles as signs of the kingdom of God.

3

The Name of Jesus Cures a Lame Man • Peter Then Calls for Repentance

One of the effects of union with Jesus is worship of God in the Jerusalem temple. Each day, at 9:00 A.M. and 3:00 P.M., sacrifices of such things as lambs, incense, wine, and flour were offered to God by the priests, accompanied by the singing and music of the Levites, and attended by Jews who could come. (An ordinary priest functioned as priest only about eight weeks of the year, unlike the high and chief priests who carried out temple responsibilities every day of the year.) It is to one of these daily afternoon services that John and Peter go, sometime after Pentecost.

Luke knows of a gate among the many gates of the temple known as the Beautiful Gate; it is doubtful that he knew exactly where it was, and we certainly do not, but it is enough for his story that it was an entrance for many into the temple building where the sacrifices were to be offered—a good place for a beggar to beg. The scheme or form in which the event is now told is typical of so many stories in the ancient literatures when dealing with a miraculous cure. Details about the man concern only his ailment and the difficulty of its cure; the story accentuates the method of cure and the fact of it; the crowd reflects the wonder and joy of the cure and thereby underlines its reality.

With fine dramatic writing Luke leads up to the main point of the story: it is in the name of Jesus Christ the Nazarene that this lame man now walks. Indeed, had not Luke

3 Now Peter and John were going up to the temple at the hour of prayer, the ninth hour. ²And a man lame from birth was being carried, whom they laid daily at that gate of the temple which is called Beautiful to ask alms of those who entered the temple. ³Seeing Peter and John about to go into the temple, he asked for alms. ⁴And Peter directed his gaze at him, with John, and said, "Look at us." ⁵And he fixed his attention upon them, expecting to receive something from them. ⁶But Peter said, "I have no silver and gold, but I give you what I have; in the name of Jesus Christ of Nazareth, walk." ⁷And he took him by the right hand and raised him up; and immediately his feet and ankles were made strong. ⁸And leaping up he stood and walked and entered the temple with them, walking and leaping and praising God. ⁹And all the people saw him walking and praising God, ¹⁰and recognized him as the one who sat for alms at the Beautiful Gate of the temple; and they were filled with wonder and amazement at what had happened to him.

11 While he clung to Peter and John, all the people ran together to them in the portico called Solomon's, astounded. ¹²And when Peter saw it he addressed the people, "Men of Israel, why do you wonder at this, or why do you stare at us, as though by our own power or piety we had made him walk? ¹³The God of Abraham and of Isaac and of Jacob, the God of our fathers, glorified his servant Jesus, whom you delivered up and denied in the presence of Pilate, when he had decided to release him. ¹⁴But you denied the Holy and Righteous One, and asked for a murderer to be granted to you, ¹⁵and killed the

Author of life, whom God raised from the dead. To this we are witnesses. [16]And his name, by faith in his name, has made this man strong whom you see and know; and the faith which is through Jesus has given the man this perfect health in the presence of you all.

17 "And now, brethren, I know that you acted in ignorance, as did also your rulers. [18]But what God foretold by the mouth of all the prophets, that his Christ should suffer, he thus fulfilled. [19]Repent therefore, and turn again, that your sins may be blotted out, that times of refreshing may come from the presence of the Lord, [20]and that he may send the Christ appointed for you, Jesus, [21]whom heaven must receive until the time for establishing all that God spoke by the mouth of his holy prophets from of old. [22]Moses said, 'The Lord God will raise up for you a prophet from your brethren as he raised me up. You shall listen to him in whatever he tells you. [23]And it shall be that every soul that does not listen to that prophet shall be destroyed from the people.' [24]And all the prophets who have spoken, from Samuel and those who came afterwards, also proclaimed these days. [25]You are the sons of the prophets and of the covenant which God gave to your fathers, saying to Abraham, 'And in your posterity shall all the families of the earth be blessed.' [26]God, having raised up his servant, sent him to you first, to bless you in turning every one of you from your wickedness."

just gone to great lengths in the Pentecost story to underline
the belief that one can be saved by calling on the name of
the Lord Jesus? In this cure story there is question only of
physical saving, but, as the Gospel has argued, physical saving is only one of the types of saving in which God is
interested.

That Peter appeals to the name of Jesus for a cure indicates that, for Peter, Jesus is alive and, if a healing is to be
done, that it will be done by Jesus. It is important to realize
in what way this kind of miracle is thought to work; the
basis of it is rooted in Jesus' own public life. When Jesus
was on earth, he often cured or healed because he was asked
to, because someone called on him, called his name and
asked for a miracle. Now he is not physically present; yet,
if one will call on his name, as in the past, he will respond
with his healing power. Thus, there is no magic here; to call
on the name of Jesus is a formula for calling on the living
Jesus at the right hand of his Father; it is he, not his name,
that hears and cures. Indeed, in this and in so many other
ways Jesus, though physically absent from this age, continues
his work as the saving Lord and Messiah. Acts is filled with
this belief.

The man is cured; indeed, by his jumping around he
suggests to some that phrase from Isaiah concerning Israel
restored to a happy life: "Yahweh is coming to save you . . .
the lame shall leap like a deer" (Is 35:4-6). The crowd con-
firms that there is no human explanation for what it has
seen.

To the portico of Solomon, a protected walkway on the
inside of the eastern wall which surrounds the temple
grounds, come many of the crowd who witnessed this miracle; evidently these people hang on to Peter and John because they think the miracle is attributable to them alone.
To dispel this thought Peter begins a speech; the speech,

however, hopes to do more than identify the miracle-worker
as Jesus.

To argue that Jesus did the miracle rather than they
would not serve Luke's purpose; he had already made clear
in his story that Jesus performed the healing. What Luke
wants to convey, first, is that the healing was done by the
one whom his audience had called guilty, when pagans had
said he was innocent, the one whom their own God had
raised from the dead, the one whom they called unjust, a
criminal worthy of death, but who was the just one, the holy
one, author of life (e.g., life to the limbs of this lame man),
the one to whom they preferred a murderer. In this particular way of presenting Jesus the healer, Peter not only identifies Jesus as the miracle-worker, but underlines his
relationship with God and the terrible mistake his audience
has made regarding Jesus. Despite their antipathy to Jesus,
it is only by faith in him that this man stands cured.

Given the attention to Jewish guilt over a Jesus who is
alive and saving with divine power, it is only logical that
Peter enters into the final goal of his speech: repentance.
Peter leads into the appeal for repentance by suggesting that
those who were responsible for putting Jesus to death did
not really know what they were doing (as Jesus had argued
on his cross). With this cure, however, and the fact of the
resurrection, the sitting at the right hand of the Father, Pentecost, the life of the followers of Jesus—in light of all this,
Peter's audience is better informed and able to make a
proper judgment about Jesus. There is now good reason to
hope that they will repent and change their minds.

Is Peter asking here that the crowd repent for its rejection of Jesus, or is he asking, in the manner of Jesus, that
the crowd repent for its various sins (one of which is the
rejection of God's Beloved)? It is not altogether certain
which is the correct answer, but the second choice seems

more likely. That is, Peter is not simply interested in re-
pairing what had gone wrong in the past; rather, he continues to represent the preaching Jesus whose message
included the call to repentance for things that had nothing
to do with his death. Peter, in other words, is offering on
behalf of Jesus salvation to this group; the forgiveness of
their sins, however, will follow only on their baptism into
the name of Jesus, just as, in the public life of Jesus, salvation
came only by following Jesus' interpretation of the mind of
God.

In light of this interpretation we can understand key
phrases of the speech. The God of "our" ancestors *glorified*
his child or servant: i.e., God *raised up from the dead* the
servant that Isaiah had said would die for our sins, though
he was himself innocent. Indeed, it is this being alive that
allows Jesus to work this cure, as it is this cure which argues
that Jesus is alive. Moses had said that God would *raise up*
a prophet who must be listened to; this "raising up" includes
that raising which is from the dead, and this live Jesus must
now be listened to. The prophets foretold *these days*; "these
days" are not just the days of Jesus' public life, but the days
of his risen life as well. God sent Jesus *first* to the Jews, but
this "first';' did not end with Jesus' death, but continues on
till the death of Stephen (Acts 7). *"God raised up his servant
to bless you by turning you from your wicked ways"*, this
"raising up" for the blessing of repentance refers not just to
God's efforts to reach his people during Jesus' public life,
but also to his efforts to reach them *now*, with Jesus alive
again to bless them. Because of his resurrection Jesus is
again the one who blesses, who, through his representatives,
works for the repentance of his people. The life of saving
continues!

Why did Peter attach this call to repentance to his explanation of a physical cure? Because the physical cure is

part of that entire cure, that radical cure that Jesus seeks through repentance. Physical cure is the sign of a deeper cure, of a more thorough saving. To see one is to be encouraged that the miracle-worker can work the greater salvation, the most fundamental of cures, upon which rests one's entry into God's presence forever.

It was a Jewish belief or hope that repentance for sins would move God to send the Messiah sooner than planned, for his people are now ready to stand in his presence. This is incorporated into the speech as a motive for repentance; to the repentant God would send refreshments in this wicked world—and eventually the Messiah himself who is waiting only for the restoration involved in repentance and forgiveness. Peter's audience should rejoice at all that is being offered them, for what their forefathers could only hope for is now theirs—and through them the entire world can enjoy the fulfillment of what people knew earlier only as promises. Through Jesus is salvation possible.

4

The Disciples, Like Jesus, On Trial • *The Community's Prayer* • *Life in the Community* • *Barnabas Introduced*

The cure of the lame man at the Beautiful Gate of the temple continues to have its repercussions. While Peter and John continue to talk about Jesus with their audience, there appear temple guards to arrest them; these are the same kind of police that arrested Jesus. One of the main motives for this arrest was the preaching of a Jesus who was resurrected from the dead; Sadducees never wanted the resurrection from the dead taught anywhere, but particularly in the temple area and especially about the Jesus whom they had helped crucify. The disciples are arrested and held overnight.

Luke's "rulers, elders and scribes" is another formula for the Sanhedrin, that supreme legislative, executive and judicial group of seventy (plus the high priest, its *ex-officio* president) which governed all Israelite matters. That the disciples remind one of Jesus who had to face the Sanhedrin is not accidental. The particular names Luke gives here (Annas, Caiaphas, Jonathan, Alexander) are historical and powerful men in Jerusalem; they were all part of one family, which is the formula for the handing on or inheriting of the high priestly office at this time.

The trial of John and Peter is ultimately ineffectual, for the disciples continue to do what they think they should do, despite the discontent of the Sanhedrin and the whipping the disciples must undergo as "disturbers of the peace." One factor which restrains the anger of the Sanhedrin is the

SCRIPTURE TEXT

4 And as they were speaking to the people, the priests and the captain of the temple and the Sadducees came upon them, ²annoyed because they were teaching the people and proclaiming in Jesus the resurrection from the dead. ³And they arrested them and put them in custody until the morrow, for it was already evening. ⁴But many of those who heard the word believed; and the number of the men came to about five thousand.

5 On the morrow their rulers and elders and scribes were gathered together in Jerusalem, ⁶with Annas the high priest and Caiaphas and John and Alexander, and all who were of the high-priestly family. ⁷And when they had set them in the midst, they inquired, "By what power or by what name did you do this?" ⁸Then Peter, filled with the Holy Spirit, said to them, "Rulers of the people and elders, ⁹if we are being examined today concerning a good deed done to a cripple, by what means this man has been healed, ¹⁰be it known to you all, and to all the people of Israel, that by the name of Jesus Christ of Nazareth, whom you crucified, whom God raised from the dead, by him this man is standing before you well. ¹¹This is the stone which was rejected by you builders, but which has become the head of the corner. ¹²And there is salvation in no one else, for there is no other name under heaven given among men by which we must be saved."

13 Now when they saw the boldness of Peter and John, and perceived that they were uneducated, common men, they wondered; and they recognized that they had been with Jesus. ¹⁴But seeing the man that had been

healed standing beside them, they had nothing to say in opposition. [15]But when they had commanded them to go aside out of the council, they conferred with one another, [16]saying, "What shall we do with these men? For that a notable sign has been performed through them is manifest to all the inhabitants of Jerusalem, and we cannot deny it. [17]But in order that it may spread no further among the people, let us warn them to speak no more to any one in this name." [18]So they called them and charged them not to speak or teach at all in the name of Jesus. [19]But Peter and John answered them, "Whether it is right in the sight of God to listen to you rather than to God, you must judge; [20]for we cannot but speak of what we have seen and heard." [21]And when they had further threatened them, they let them go, finding no way to punish them, because of the people; for all men praised God for what had happened. [22]For the man on whom this sign of healing was performed was more than forty years old.

23 When they were released they went to their friends and reported what the chief priests and the elders had said to them. [24]And when they heard it, they lifted their voices together to God and said, "Sovereign Lord, who didst make the heaven and the earth and the sea and everything in them, [25]who by the mouth of our father David, thy servant, didst say by the Holy Spirit,

'Why did the Gentiles rage,
and the peoples imagine vain things?
[26]The kings of the earth set themselves in array,
and the rulers were gathered together,
against the Lord and against his Anointed'—
[27]for truly in this city there were gathered together against thy holy servant Jesus, whom thou didst anoint, both Herod and Pontius Pilate, with the Gentiles and the

peoples of Israel, [28]to do whatever thy hand and thy plan had predestined to take place. [29]And now, Lord, look upon their threats, and grant to thy servants to speak thy word with all boldness, [30]while thou stretchest out thy hand to heal, and signs and wonders are performed through the name of thy holy servant Jesus." [31]And when they had prayed, the place in which they were gathered together was shaken; and they were all filled with the Holy Spirit and spoke the word of God with boldness.

32 Now the company of those who believed were of one heart and soul, and no one said that any of the things which he possessed was his own, but they had everything in common. [33]And with great power the apostles gave their testimony to the resurrection of the Lord Jesus, and great grace was upon them all. [34]There was not a needy person among them, for as many as were possessors of lands or houses sold them, and brought the proceeds of what was sold [35]and laid it at the apostles' feet; and distribution was made to each as any had need. [36]Thus Joseph who was surnamed by the apostles Barnabas (which means, Son of encouragement), a Levite, a native of Cyprus, [37]sold a field which belonged to him, and brought the money and laid it at the apostles' feet.

good will the disciples enjoy with the ordinary people; as with Jesus (except at the trial before Pilate), the people are greatly taken with these preachers, and give them support and encouragement, if not conversion to belief in Jesus.

This first trial of the disciples (there will soon be another arrest and another trial) gives Luke the opportunity to emphasize a number of important points. Luke had quoted Jesus (Lk 12:4-12) that the disciples should not, in times of trials to come, "worry about how to defend yourselves or what to say, for the Holy Spirit will teach you what to say." Here we have the first of many times when the Spirit enlightens and strengthens the disciples in time of trial; Acts completes the Gospel, as Luke had planned.

the Sanhedrin gives Peter the opportunity to speak again the thoughts which dominated a great part of his speech Luke gave us in chapter 3; even the way the Sanhedrin introduces the subject is opportune: "By what power, in whose name have you cured this man?" This question gives Peter (and Luke) the occasion to restate in the most forceful terms one will find in Acts or in the Gospel that this cure, and salvation in its deepest significance, can only come through the person designated by God: Jesus Christ, the Nazarene. Peter, true to the early form of Luke's chapters here, affirms that the death prescribed for Jesus is replaced by his being raised from the dead as the true sign of his relationship with God. Finally, Luke again cites what must have been a much-used line of Psalm 118 (v 22) in Christian application of the Old Testament: the stone rejected (by Israel) has been made the very cornerstone (by God of his people). Jesus had said in one of his parables (Lk 22:17) that this psalm verse would come true; now, Luke notes, it has.

The way Luke tells this story keeps in the forefront of the reader's mind the objective reality of a lame man who is cured. As in so many other places, Luke here insists on things heard and on things seen as the grounding of Christian belief. Acceptance or rejection of Jesus is to start from facts known to many, many people.

The solution of the Sanhedrin, now fearful of the people and unable to deny the miracle worked, is to prohibit these men ever to represent Jesus in public again. This prohibition sets the stage for the next arrest of the disciples and gives Peter and John another opportunity to argue the Christian case: theirs is a mission from God, and that is not something human prohibitions will stop. But Peter repeats again the challenge to all those who doubt: he is speaking and proclaiming only what he has seen and heard.

Luke now notes the age of the man cured by Jesus, as if not only to accentuate the power of the miracle and give good reason why the people praise God so heartily, but also to indicate that the story of the cured man has come to an end.

Attention now turns, as Luke directs it, to the prayer which sums up the community's reactions to what had happened to Peter and John. This prayer reminds God of his own words concerning Jesus, his Anointed, and interprets those words as prophecy about Herod Antipas, Pontius Pilate and the people of Israel: they conspired against God and his Anointed. What they did to Jesus is, however, nothing different, as Luke has always insisted, than what God had known would happen and had planned for. But why does their prayer at the story of Peter and John make them think of what happened to Jesus? The answer lies in the fact that they consider themselves to be the continuation of and imitators of Jesus: what happened to God's *servant* Jesus now happens to his *servants*, the Christians. It is within this continuity that they ask that they be empowered still further, like Jesus of old, to proclaim the word of God. They ask for those miracles and signs which the Christians came to un-

derstand to be supportive of the preaching (and thus not
equal to the preaching), miracles and signs to be worked
by God through his holy servant, Jesus. This kind of prayer
underlines the continuity of preaching and life-experience
between Jesus, the Master and Lord, and his committed followers. The Christian community has always considered itself in this way.

Luke's description of God's response to this prayer intentionally evokes the memory of the great Pentecost. As
with the Pentecost which began all other Pentecosts, the
effect of the Spirit is to proclaim the word of God coura-
geously. In Acts, particularly in its first chapters, one is always certain of what one is not always certain of in the
twentieth century: the will and action of God.

At this point Luke writes another generalized description of the Christians in Jerusalem, rather than continue with
a concrete episode. Here we learn again of the intense unity
these early Christians feel among themselves and, in the
spirit of their recent prayer, of the continual witness to the
resurrection of Jesus, whom they know as their Lord. To
witness to his resurrection is the key to accepting all that
Jesus had preached and taught: he must be alive, he must
be brought to life by the love of God. This witnessing to
Jesus' being raised is supported and confirmed by miracles,
as they had asked. Once again Luke impresses on the reader
the tribute ordinary people paid to the truth of the Christian
belief: all were held in great esteem and respect—a very
good argument in favor of Christianity.

Stress here is put upon that charity which showed itself
in giving up one's goods to rid another of want; how often
had Jesus exhorted people not to let wealth and poverty
separate people from love of one another, not to let wealth
dictate one's life rather than God. At the moment it is a small
detail to say that what was sold was given to the apostles

who then would be the distributors of goods to those in need; but this small detail will have its part to play more than once, and very soon.

To speak now of generous people is Luke's own cue to himself to introduce the generous Barnabas, whose original name was Joseph and who originally came from Cyprus. This is the Barnabas who will play such an important role as guide to the newly baptized Paul and co-apostle with him in parts of present-day Turkey. For now, he exemplifies the generosity typical of one dedicated here in Jerusalem to Jesus. He, like others at this time, lives out what Jesus preached and lives as Jesus lived. The community, too, in its own way *witnesses* to Jesus.

5

Sin Against the Holy Spirit • Miracles Lead to Imprisonment, Then to Trial and Advice of Gamaliel

The story of Ananias and Sapphira shows that not all Christians lived up to the tone that has been set since the outpouring of the Holy Spirit; from the looks of things, though, Ananias and Sapphira are the exception to the rule. Ironically, their difficulty centers on wealth, on possessions. Though the story is simply told, with obvious contrast drawn between this husband and wife and Barnabas and the Christians in general, some particularized comments are appropriate.

The precise sin of Ananias and Sapphira is not greed, or any other sin associated with their not sharing their possessions with the needy; presumably, a story dealing with covetousness would not merit such prominence as does this story. The sin of Ananias and Sapphira lies in their having promised something to the Holy Spirit, only not to give it: their lie is to God, not to men. They have put the Spirit of God to the test.

It is against such a formidable evil that the rest of the story makes sense. The penalty for sinning against the Spirit is death; Jesus had earlier warned against the sins against the Spirit and their unforgivableness (Lk 12:10). The Old Testament is filled with stories which, like this one, are meant to underline, even at the expense of concern for mercy, the seriousness and viciousness of sins so directly against God. One can argue that such stories (cf. Paul's recital in I Cor

SCRIPTURE TEXT

5 But a man named Ananias with his wife Sapphira sold a piece of property, [2]and with his wife's knowledge he kept back some of the proceeds, and brought only a part and laid it at the apostles' feet. [3]But Peter said, "Ananias, why has Satan filled your heart to lie to the Holy Spirit and to keep back part of the proceeds of the land? [4]While it remained unsold, did it not remain your own? And after it was sold, was it not at your disposal? How is it that you have contrived this deed in your heart? You have not lied to men but to God." [5]When Ananias heard these words, he fell down and died. And great fear came upon all who heard of it. [6]The young men rose and wrapped him up and carried him out and buried him.

7 After an interval of about three hours his wife came in, not knowing what had happened. [8]And Peter said to her, "Tell me whether you sold the land for so much." And she said, "Yes, for so much." [9]But Peter said to her, "How is it that you have agreed together to tempt the Spirit of the Lord? Hark, the feet of those that have buried your husband are at the door, and they will carry you out." [10]Immediately she fell down at his feet and died. When the young men came in they found her dead, and they carried her out and buried her beside her husband. [11]And great fear came upon the whole church, and upon all who heard of these things.

12 Now many signs and wonders were done among the people by the hands of the apostles. And they were all together in Solomon's Portico. [13]None of the rest dared join them, but the people held them in high honor. [14]And more than ever believers were added to the Lord,

multitudes both of men and women, [15]so that they even carried out the sick into the streets, and laid them on beds and pallets, that as Peter came by at least his shadow might fall on some of them. [16]The people also gathered from the towns around Jerusalem, bringing the sick and those afflicted with unclean spirits, and they were all healed.

17 But the high priest rose up and all who were with him, that is, the party of the Sadducees, and filled with jealousy [18]they arrested the apostles and put them in the common prison. [19]But at night an angel of the Lord opened the prison doors and brought them out and said, [20]"Go and stand in the temple and speak to the people all the words of this Life." [21]And when they heard this, they entered the temple at daybreak and taught.

Now the high priest came and those who were with him and called together the council and all the senate of Israel, and sent to the prison to have them brought. [22]But when the officers came, they did not find them in the prison, and they returned and reported, [23]"We found the prison securely locked and the sentries standing at the doors, but when we opened it we found no one inside." [24]Now when the captain of the temple and the chief priests heard these words, they were much perplexed about them, wondering what this would come to. [25]And some one came and told them, "The men whom you put in prison are standing in the temple and teaching the people." [26]Then the captain with the officers went and brought them, but without violence, for they were afraid of being stoned by the people.

27 And when they had brought them, they set them before the council. And the high priest questioned them, [28]saying, "We strictly charged you not to teach in this name, yet here you have filled Jerusalem with your

teaching and you intend to bring this man's blood upon us." 29But Peter and the apostles answered, "We must obey God rather than men. 30The God of our fathers raised Jesus whom you killed by hanging him on a tree. 31God exalted him at his right hand as Leader and Savior, to give repentance to Israel and forgiveness of sins. 32And we are witnesses to these things, and so is the Holy Spirit whom God has given to those who obey him."

33 When they heard this they were enraged and wanted to kill them. 34But a Pharisee in the council named Gamaliel, a teacher of the law, held in honor by all the people, stood up and ordered the men to be put outside for a while. 35And he said to them, "Men of Israel, take care what you do with these men. 36For before these days Theudas arose, giving himself out to be somebody, and a number of men, about four hundred, joined him; but he was slain and all who followed him were dispersed and came to nothing. 37After him Judas the Galilean arose in the days of the census and drew away some of the people after him; he also perished, and all who followed him were scattered. 38So in the present case I tell you, keep away from these men and let them alone; for if this plan or this undertaking is of men, it will fail; 39but if it is of God, you will not be able to overthrow them. You might even be found opposing God!"

40 So they took his advice, and when they had called in the apostles, they beat them and charged them not to speak in the name of Jesus, and let them go. 41Then they left the presence of the council, rejoicing that they were counted worthy to suffer dishonor for the name. 42And every day in the temple and at home they did not cease teaching and preaching Jesus as the Christ.

10:5–11) present only part of the reality of things, and thus a distortion of the fuller reality. But in the centuries of Luke's experience, such stories were understood to be legitimate ways of teaching vital lessons about the truth of one's actions and their merits. The lesson here is that, with every hope that God will be merciful, the natural result of this sin is death.

It is in accord with the seriousness of the sin that the personality of Peter is depicted here; it is also noteworthy that not only are outsiders profoundly stunned by this death, but so is the Church itself deeply impressed by it.

After this lesson, Luke presents the Christians in their usual place (along the eastern wall of the temple grounds) and in their usual spirit of harmony, respected by non-believers. Luke here stresses, among the elements he often uses to describe generalized pictures of the Christian community, the powers of curing exercised by the apostles. These were recently prayed for by the whole community; they are again described in those words which have been used of Jesus' miracles and of those worked by Aaron and Moses for the earlier salvation of God's people from Egypt: these are the "signs" and "wonders" of God. In reading of the powers of the apostles and especially of Peter, one cannot help but be reminded of Jesus who, upon simply being touched, cured the sick.

Such curing of all the sickly caused jealousy among the Sadducees (who knew these cures were used to argue that Jesus had been raised from the dead), and the high priest concurred. The apostles are arrested, only to be freed by the angel of the Lord, a figure famous in the Old Testament as the expression of God's saving power against limits insuperable for human beings. It is clear, from Luke's details, that the continuance of the salvific preaching is indomitable; nothing can stop the will of God.

Here for the first time the Christian life is referred to as a "Way." This term was used by other religious groups about their own understandings of how life was to be lived. Perhaps the Christians used it about themselves because they saw themselves, like their Lord in Galilee, to be on their way to the right hand of the Father by performing those deeds which befit repentance and forgiveness and the gift of the Spirit.

To the wonderment of the Sanhedrin, grouped now to judge these disciples, word is first brought that the jail is empty—a clear sign of the power of God over human locks and chains. The reader is to take satisfaction in his own knowledge of these happenings and in the confusion and consternation of the Sanhedrin. The miracle of liberation is now dropped from consideration, though a certain logic might say that disinterest in the disciples' getting out of a jail which is heavily guarded and thoroughly locked is il-logical. The only purpose of the miracle, however, was to show the powerlessness of the highest authorities to impede God's will; in that, the story has succeeded—and for Luke that is logic enough.

The trial now gives Peter and the others a chance to continue the proclamation begun after the cure of the lame man at the Beautiful Gate and developed in their first trial; this unity of preaching is organized by Luke from his sources.

The brief speech of Peter underlines the belief that what is happening is due to God, and therefore must be gone along with. Peter again repeats what has become the nutshell of the argument: God continues to save through Jesus, because, despite even his death, God insists that through him comes salvation; the resurrection proves this. Peter notes that "the God of our forefathers" has acted on behalf of Jesus; by using this terminology Peter's audience

is set at odds with its forefathers—the audience is the out-
sider, not Jesus. To say that Jesus was put to death "by hanging on a tree" is to indicate that Jesus was considered to be
a criminal whose very corpse would pollute the land of Israel, if it were not buried on the day of death (cf. Dt 21:23).
Such language clearly marks the difference of attitude, on
the part of God and on the part of the Sanhedrin, with regard
to Jesus.

God has glorified Jesus through resurrection and ascension. But this raising up in glory is to be understood as God's
way of allowing Jesus to continue in power his activity as
leader and Savior, through the plea for repentance and the
assuredness of forgiveness of sins for Israel. To all this these
men on trial function as witnesses only; but with them in
witness is the very Spirit of God who is filling those who
respond favorably to Jesus' leadership and saving plea.

It is significant that at this point in the narrative the
suggestion of death for the apostles is expressed; the penalty
corresponds to the fact that, with this speech of Peter, the
first part of Acts—"to be my witnesses in Jerusalem"—is
now coming to an end. There remains only the condem-
natory speech of Stephen and the mission to Jerusalem will
be complete.

Death, however, was not the actual punishment given
the apostles. Gamaliel, well-known even outside Christian
writings as a great Pharisee and teacher in Judaism (even to
teaching Paul before he became a Christian), suggests a way
of approaching this "Christian" problem that Luke hopes
other rulers throughout the Mediterranean of his time will
adopt. In brief, the argument breaks things down into halves:
if God is for them, we cannot stop them; if God is not for
them, they will fall on their faces (without our having to
get involved and thereby stir up the common people against
us).

Not death, but the usual "flogging" for having disturbed the peace—this is the punishment for the apostles. And it is welcomed by them, no doubt as a fulfillment of Jesus' words (Lk 6:22–23) and as an opportunity to suffer for their leader (something they could not bring themselves to do after Jesus' capture in Gethsemane).

They plugged on, proclaiming publicly and privately the good news rooted in this Jesus Christ; as with Paul at the end of Luke's work, they preached unhindered. But for some of the Christians, there will arise hindrance—such opposition as will drive them out of Israel—and thereby bring the Christian preaching into the vaster world of the Mediterranean. Luke will now introduce these Christians to us.

6

The Seven Take Over Some of the Duties of the Twelve • Stephen Preaches, Is Put on Trial

In the first century A.D., it was not very easy for women to work in the public arenas to earn money for their support; for such income, most depended totally on their husbands, sons and/or male relatives. Thus, when a woman was widowed, her financial situation became precarious. It is not surprising, then, to find that the Mosaic law stirred in a particular way the sympathies of religious Jews to form agencies which would consistently provide widows with the necessities of life. Nor is it surprising that the Jews who became Christians followed the same expression of love for neighbors; they, too, created formal means to feed those who could hardly feed themselves. It is about this care for widows that Luke now writes.

A difficulty has arisen concerning a breakdown in the distribution of food to Hellenist widows. These ladies are widows, Jewish, Christians; why are they called Hellenist? For many Jews, to come to Jerusalem to live was at best an unfulfilled dream, but some did, at the end of their working lives, have the means to leave their Mediterranean homes to enter Israel and live out their final days in the shadow of God's house. It is of course natural, upon reflection, to see how these people, though Jews, would tend to congregate together and live separately from those Jews who were native to Israel and to Jerusalem. Many customs were different, and language was notably different; those who had spent their entire lives in societies dominated by Greek and Ro-

6 Now in these days when the disciples were increasing in number, the Hellenists murmured against the Hebrews because their widows were neglected in the daily distribution. [2]And the twelve summoned the body of the disciples and said, "It is not right that we should give up preaching the word of God to serve tables. [3]Therefore, brethren, pick out from among you seven men of good repute, full of the Spirit and of wisdom, whom we may appoint to this duty. [4]But we will devote ourselves to prayer and to the ministry of the word." [5]And what they said pleased the whole multitude, and they chose Stephen, a man full of faith and of the Holy Spirit, and Philip, and Prochorus, and Nicanor, and Timon, and Parmenas, and Nicolaus, a proselyte of Antioch. [6]These they set before the apostles, and they prayed and laid their hands upon them.

7 And the word of God increased; and the number of the disciples multiplied greatly in Jerusalem, and a great many of the priests were obedient to the faith.

8 And Stephen, full of grace and power, did great wonders and signs among the people. [9]Then some of those who belonged to the synagogue of the Freedmen (as it was called), and of the Cyrenians, and of the Alexandrians, and of those from Cilicia and Asia, arose and disputed with Stephen. [10]But they could not withstand the wisdom and the Spirit with which he spoke. [11]Then they secretly instigated men, who said, "We have heard him speak blasphemous words against Moses and God." [12]And they stirred up the people and the elders and the scribes, and they came upon him and seized him and

brought him before the council, [13]and set up false witnesses who said, "This man never ceases to speak words against this holy place and the law; [14]for we have heard him say that this Jesus of Nazareth will destroy this place, and will change the customs which Moses delivered to us." [15]And gazing at him, all who sat in the council saw that his face was like the face of an angel.

man cultures brought their customs with them, and the Greek language as well. Even in their studies of the Jewish law and in their prayers in common in the synagogues, these Hellenists formed their own synagogues (in Jerusalem alone about this time there were, according to some ancient testimonies, over two hundred synagogues—it took only nine willing men to form a synagogue, where one prayed and studied, but did not offer sacrifice).

The Hellenists by and large arrived in Jerusalem in the later years of their lives; presumably, in most cases the man was the older, and thus died sooner than his partner, leaving her a widow without much income. For some reason, the Hellenists who had become Christians (cf. the kinds of Jews who were present at Pentecost, living in Jerusalem, but from all over the Mediterranean) suffered after a while in the formal distribution of food which was organized by the native Jewish Christians. The solution to this malfunction was to make Hellenists part of the team responsible for the distribution of food; taking managerial responsibility should smooth out the wrinkles.

Apparently, the Twelve, at whose feet many laid the money coming from the sale of their goods for the support of their fellow Christians, were responsible for the distribution of food to all the needy. With the help of the Hellenists, who would choose men "of good reputation, filled with the Holy Spirit and with wisdom," and in an atmosphere of prayer, the Twelve, through a concrete ceremony, transfer to seven men the responsibility for this service. From the way in which the Twelve express themselves, one might conclude that the Hellenist Seven took over the entire distribution of food, to Palestinian and to Hellenist Jewish Christian widows; the Twelve want to be free to do all the preaching they possibly can, for they are the eye-witnesses on whom the preaching in the main depends.

Chosen by the entire assembly for this service (the Greek word to "serve" is *diakonein*—hence, *deacon*) are two men in particular who will play significant parts in Acts: Stephen, whom we will now consider, and Philip, who is the preacher of Christianity to the Samaritans after the death of Stephen. The problem, then, is resolved for these widows, and the word of the Lord continues to spread and win over believers to it; even priests begin to accept Jesus as their Lord.

The fact that Stephen succeeded the Twelve in one area of service seems enough to have him introduced as a co-worker in another area: Stephen, like the Twelve, is filled with the Holy Spirit and begins to work those miracles which are described as "signs and wonders." It is not said that Stephen was the equal of the Twelve; yet, the description of him suggests that, at last, we meet those who preach, not as eye-witnesses, but as trustworthy witnesses taught by the Twelve. The reliability of the Hellenists, who were not companions of Jesus, yet represent him, is a quality Luke absolutely insists was real. As the Twelve learned from Jesus, so Stephen learned from the Twelve.

Stephen, a Hellenist, is challenged in his beliefs by Hellenists who are not Christians. Luke notes that they are from Cyrene and Alexandria (thus, from Africa) and from Cilicia and Asia (now modern Turkey). As with so many other Jews, these had their own synagogue, called the Synagogue of the Freedmen, perhaps a reference to those Jews who had been taken to Rome as slaves after a Roman conquest (e.g., 63 B.C.), earned their freedom there, and then returned to Jerusalem. That Stephen is not involved with Palestinian Jews suggests that the kind of argument he engaged in was particular to Jewish Hellenists. Certainly, these Jews had had their own experience of Judaism—they had lived among pagans, which those Jews who had spent their lives in Israel and particularly in Jerusalem would not have had. These Hellenist Jews surely had a great devotion to Jerusalem, for they worked hard to return to the city; yet, their understanding of temple and Mosaic customs might be such as to make their disagreements with Stephen arguments which were peculiar to Hellenists.

In any event, the strength of Stephen, who, as Jesus had said, was fortified in his defense of Jesus by the Spirit, overpowered all opponents; this led his enemies to bring him to trial before those who had condemned both Jesus and the apostles; the witnesses seem destined to follow the fate of their Lord.

The Sanhedrin received the prisoner and heard the charges; as in the trial of Jesus, some of these charges are false, none of them convincing. But these charges are not simply grounds for an unjust condemnation of one witness. They are two considerations of such religious and theological significance that they must be treated by Luke in an explicit way, if he is to show Theophilus how it is that the religion Theophilus has been taught is a religion without the temple and without many of the Mosaic laws and customs. To this end, what were very broadly stated accusations are ultimately reduced to rather concrete charges: Stephen is accused of saying that Jesus of Nazareth will destroy the temple and will change the traditions handed down by Moses. The element of the Christian community which was Jewish did not, at this early stage of Christianity, preach such beliefs with insistence; these Christians knew Jesus had wept over Jerusalem and regretted its rejection of him, and knew what historically happened to Jerusalem for its rejection of God's messengers. They also knew, from Jesus' arguments with Jewish religious authorities, that he felt free to alter the Mosaic laws and traditions as he thought fit. It would fall to a Hellenist, however, to take a more critical stance

toward the temple and the customs which he had lived without for many years or had to adjust to in his life among the
pagans. Indeed, it seems that it is this Hellenist Jewish mind
which was able to adjust to a new way of relating to God,
a way without temple and many of the Mosaic prescriptions
and their interpretations; this group seems to have been
more alert to the way in which God was dealing with Gentiles and open to the implications of their conversions.

Stephen now answers the charge regarding the temple.
It is in chapter 15 that Luke will answer the charge about
the law.

7

Stephen's Defense and Death • *The Emergence of Saul*

There is no universal agreement as to the interpretation of Stephen's speech; a good number of scholars maintain that it does not answer the accusations made against Stephen and that there is no total unity or coherence to the speech. The interpretation given here sees the speech as coherent and unified and a direct answer to the charges laid against Stephen.

The speech of Stephen is divided into five panels; these are: (1) the story of Abraham, (2) the story of Joseph, (3) the story of Moses, (4) the story of David and Solomon and the temple, and (5) the accusation of hardheartedness and deafness to the Spirit of God made against Stephen's hearers. Let us see how these five panels fit together.

The story of Abraham begins with the call of Abraham to leave his country to go to the promised land; the story ends with the assurance that Abraham's children will one day actually live in the land (once freed from Egypt). The purpose behind this movement to Israel is the culminating point of the Abraham story: they will be set free so that they might worship God in this place (= the temple of Jerusalem). Israel's reason for being, then, is the worship of God in the temple.

The story of Joseph in Egypt highlights one idea, as did the story of Abraham; however, whereas the Abraham story underlined worship of Yahweh, the Joseph story emphasizes a savior of Israel. Joseph is that person who, though rejected

7 And the high priest said, "Is this so?" [2]And Stephen said:

"Brethren and fathers, hear me. The God of glory appeared to our father Abraham, when he was in Mesopotamia, before he lived in Haran, [3]and said to him, 'Depart from your land and from your kindred and go into the land which I will show you.' [4]Then he departed from the land of the Chaldeans, and lived in Haran. And after his father died, God removed him from there into this land in which you are now living; [5]yet he gave him no inheritance in it, not even a foot's length, but promised to give it to him in possession and to his posterity after him, though he had no child. [6]And God spoke to this effect, that his posterity would be aliens in a land belonging to others, who would enslave them and ill-treat them four hundred years. [7]'But I will judge the nation which they serve,' said God, 'and after that they shall come out and worship me in this place.' [8]And he gave him the covenant of circumcision. And so Abraham became the father of Isaac, and circumcised him on the eighth day; and Isaac became the father of Jacob, and Jacob of the twelve patriarchs.

9 "And the patriarchs, jealous of Joseph, sold him into Egypt; but God was with him, [10]and rescued him out of all his afflictions, and gave him favor and wisdom before Pharaoh, king of Egypt, who made him governor over Egypt and over all his household. [11]Now there came a famine throughout all Egypt and Canaan, and great affliction, and our fathers could find no food. [12]But when Jacob heard that there was grain in Egypt, he sent forth

our fathers the first time. [13]And at the second visit Joseph made himself known to his brothers, and Joseph's family became known to Pharaoh. [14]And Joseph sent and called to him Jacob his father and all his kindred, seventy-five souls; [15]and Jacob went down into Egypt. And he died, himself and our fathers, [16]and they were carried back to Shechem and laid in the tomb that Abraham had bought for a sum of silver from the sons of Hamor in Shechem.

17 "But as the time of the promise drew near, which God had granted to Abraham, the people grew and multiplied in Egypt [18]till there arose over Egypt another king who had not known Joseph. [19]He dealt craftily with our race and forced our fathers to expose their infants, that they might not be kept alive. [20]At this time Moses was born, and was beautiful before God. And he was brought up for three months in his father's house; [21]and when he was exposed, Pharaoh's daughter adopted him and brought him up as her own son. [22]And Moses was instructed in all the wisdom of the Egyptians, and he was mighty in his words and deeds.

23 "When he was forty years old, it came into his heart to visit his brethren, the sons of Israel. [24]And seeing one of them being wronged, he defended the oppressed man and avenged him by striking the Egyptian. [25]He supposed that his brethren understood that God was giving them deliverance by his hand, but they did not understand. [26]And on the following day he appeared to them as they were quarreling and would have reconciled them, saying, 'Men, you are brethren, why do you wrong each other?' [27]But the man who was wronging his neighbor thrust him aside, saying, 'Who made you a ruler and a judge over us? [28]Do you want to kill me as you killed the Egyptian yesterday?' [29]At this retort Moses fled, and

became an exile in the land of Midian, where he became the father of two sons.

30 "Now when forty years had passed, an angel appeared to him in the wilderness of Mount Sinai, in a flame of fire in a bush. [31]When Moses saw it he wondered at the sight; and as he drew near to look, the voice of the Lord came, [32]'I am the God of your fathers, the God of Abraham and of Isaac and of Jacob.' And Moses trembled and did not dare to look. [33]And the Lord said to him, 'Take off the shoes from your feet, for the place where you are standing is holy ground. [34]I have surely seen the ill-treatment of my people that are in Egypt and heard their groaning, and I have come down to deliver them. And now come, I will send you to Egypt.'

35 "This Moses whom they refused, saying, 'Who made you a ruler and a judge?' God sent as both ruler and deliverer by the hand of the angel that appeared to him in the bush. [36]He led them out, having performed wonders and signs in Egypt and at the Red Sea, and in the wilderness for forty years. [37]This is the Moses who said to the Israelites, 'God will raise up for you a prophet from your brethren as he raised me up.' [38]This is he who was in the congregation in the wilderness with the angel who spoke to him at Mount Sinai, and with our fathers; and he received living oracles to give to us. [39]Our fathers refused to obey him, but thrust him aside, and in their hearts they turned to Egypt, [40]saying to Aaron, 'Make for us gods to go before us; as for this Moses who led us out from the land of Egypt, we do not know what has become of him.' [41]And they made a calf in those days, and offered a sacrifice to the idol and rejoiced in the works of their hands. [42]But God turned and gave them over to worship the host of heaven, as it is written in the book of the prophets:

'Did you offer to me slain beasts and sacrifices,
forty years in the wilderness, O house of Israel?
[43]And you took up the tent of Moloch,
and the star of the god Rephan,
the figures which you made to worship;
and I will remove you beyond Babylon.'

44 "Our fathers had the tent of witness in the wilderness, even as he who spoke to Moses directed him to make it, according to the pattern that he had seen. [45]Our fathers in turn brought it in with Joshua when they dispossessed the nations which God thrust out before our fathers. So it was until the days of David, [46]who found favor in the sight of God and asked leave to find a habitation for the God of Jacob. [47]But it was Solomon who built a house for him. [48]Yet the Most High does not dwell in houses made with hands; as the prophet says,

[49]"Heaven is my throne,
and earth my footstool.
What house will you build for me, says the Lord,
or what is the place of my rest?
[50]Did not my hand make all these things?'

51 "You stiff-necked people, uncircumcised in heart and ears, you always resist the Holy Spirit. As your fathers did, so do you. [52]Which of the prophets did not your fathers persecute? And they killed those who announced beforehand the coming of the Righteous One, whom you have now betrayed and murdered, [53]you who received the law as delivered by angels and did not keep it."

54 Now when they heard these things they were enraged, and they ground their teeth against him. [55]But he, full of the Holy Spirit, gazed into heaven and saw the glory of God, and Jesus standing at the right hand of God; [56]and he said, "Behold, I see the heavens opened, and the

Son of man standing at the right hand of God." ⁵⁷But they cried out with a loud voice and stopped their ears and rushed together upon him. ⁵⁸Then they cast him out of the city and stoned him; and the witnesses laid down their garments at the feet of a young man named Saul. ⁵⁹And as they were stoning Stephen, he prayed, "Lord Jesus, receive my spirit." ⁶⁰And he knelt down and cried with a loud voice, "Lord, do not hold this sin against them." And when he had said this, he fell asleep.

and sold by his own brothers into a slavery, turns out to be their savior. The relationship suggested between this story and the facts of Jesus' life is clear: Joseph is a foreshadowing of the savior Jesus.

The Moses story is the longest in the speech and embraces both elements brought out in the Abraham and Joseph stories; at first, Moses, like Joseph, is described by Stephen in such a way as to remind one of the Savior Jesus, but, by the end of the narrative, the emphasis has changed to underscore the false worship to which Israel commits itself in the desert. The key to the significance of the Moses story lies in the fact that Israel abandons God because it gives up on the mediator between God and man. As the text says, "We do not know where Moses is, so let us find for ourselves other gods to lead us." In doing this, is not Israel frustrating its very reason for being: the worship of Yahweh?

Many years after the desert experience, David and then Solomon assume the throne of Israel. David planned a temple; Solomon, his son, actually built it. But Stephen quotes a text from Isaiah (admittedly written centuries after the building of the temple) which finds fault, not with the temple in itself, but with Israel's misconception of it; Israel thinks of the temple as a "house" in which God is contained, and in so thinking has a false understanding of the God it is to worship. As so many other things made Israel's worship of Yahweh unacceptable, so such a gross misunderstanding of the meaning of Yahweh makes Israel's worship unacceptable. This wrong identification of God is what Stephen accuses his hearers of: they are guilty of misconceiving the very meaning of God and thus must face the realization that their worship, like that of their forefathers in the desert, is unacceptable to God. Is there any doubt now why the temple will be destroyed? Such was the accusation made against Stephen; Stephen has explained why the temple will be de-

stroyed, for Yahweh cannot accept a worship which assumes
that he is like pagan gods, who live in houses built by human
hands.

Would there actually be Jews who so misconceived
things as to think of their God as confined to a house made
by human hands, thus subjecting God to the power of human beings? Certainly this was not the thinking expressed
by the holy books of the Old Testament or by traditional
Jewish religious authority. It might, however, have been a
perception Stephen picked up from certain of those Jews
who had passed so much of their lives amidst pagan temples;
the thoughts about the gods associated with pagan temples
may have seeped into the attitude of some Jews Stephen
now contends with in Jerusalem.

As with all else in the Acts of the Apostles, so here the
argument ultimately comes down to acceptance of Jesus as
the key to knowing and pleasing God, to rejection of Jesus
as the sure way which leads to ignorance of God and to
divine anger which results in the destruction of the temple
and of Jerusalem. It is the peculiarity of the Stephen speech
that it takes up questions both of worship and of Savior,
interweaving the past of Israel in such a way as to show how
certain stages anticipated and forecast the coming of the
Savior and how other stages reveal that rejection of the mediator between God and mankind results in idol-worship;
rejection of the mediator means that Israel loses its true
understanding of God and thereby engages in a worship
which is unacceptable to God and must be punished.

With such a speech as this, Stephen, from the Hellenist
Christian view, condemns those who will not accept Jesus.
It is a speech like this which is used by Luke to give the
Christian explanation for the destruction of Jerusalem. Re-
membering that Luke is writing Acts some fifteen years after

the levelling of Jerusalem, one realizes that this tragedy can be explained within the limits of one speech, of one chapter. Not so easy to explain is the right answer for problems that still bother the Christian communities at the writing of Acts; such a problem is at the heart of the second half of the charge against Stephen: Jesus will change the customs handed down to us by Moses. Indeed, in Luke's own time there were still some difficulties in certain sectors of the Christian communities concerning the necessity of circumcision and obedience to the total law of Moses for salvation. To resolve this problem to Luke's satisfaction Luke will need more than one speech; he will need the next eight chapters!

To hear themselves once more accused of rejecting a messenger of God, now by a Hellenist only recently come to Israel, infuriates the judges, just as Peter and the apostles had infuriated them. Stephen senses what will occur and looks to his Lord. He finds him at the right hand of the Father, for there the Son of Man has taken his place in power and victorious glory. In sight of this, Stephen proceeds to die a death which can be a model for Christians after him. He is both forgiving of enemies and trusting of Jesus, to whom he commends his soul. One can hardly doubt that Luke modeled the telling of this death after the way Jesus, the Master, died; as with the case of Jesus, so here with Stephen, the kind of approach Stephen takes to death is itself an argument on behalf of his innocence.

For his identification of Jesus as the Son of Man in glory (Jesus at his own trial told these very judges that "from now on I will be at the right hand of the Father in glory") Stephen is guilty of blasphemy, the punishment for which is stoning to death. Woven into the violence is the name and person of Saul; minor is his role here, but his will coincides with those who do the stoning. He will soon have his chance to assume a major role. It all ends with death, or, better, as Luke puts it: Stephen falls asleep, someday to be awakened by the Son of Man.

With the end of Stephen's life comes the end of the formal mission to Jerusalem; now we must consider the witnessing that went on "in Judea and Samaria." As elsewhere, so here, we ask ourselves: Do we get a sense as to how Luke's narrative has given to Theophilus an ever greater awareness of how sure and reliable are the things Theophilus has been taught? The preaching is slowly, inexorably being put into the hands of others than the eye-witnesses, but Luke has shown how those who followed Christ reflect him purely and serve only to re-present him.

8

Persecution Against the Hellenist Christians • Philip Evangelizes in Samaria, Then Baptizes an African • Peter and John Correct Simon

With the death of Stephen a persecution was begun against the Hellenist Christians in Jerusalem and those who thought like them. Palestinian or Jewish "Hebrew" Christians were not persecuted, but lived on in their own style by which they integrated belief in Jesus with Jewish customs and practices. Though many of the eye-witnesses to Jesus remain in Jerusalem, the preaching there, about which Jesus spoke in Acts 1:8, is formally over. At this juncture it is worth reflecting how little Luke actually told us about what must have been years in which the Christian community grew and prospered. True, we have general descriptions or summaries sprinkled throughout the six chapters dealing with this Jerusalem period, but the actual, concrete, particularized events are few: (1) replacement of Judas, (2) Pentecost and Peter's preaching, (3) cure of the lame man and Peter's preaching, (4) arrest of Peter and his trial, (5) prayer of the community, (6) Barnabas, Ananias and Sapphira, (7) arrest and trial of Peter, (8) appointment of seven, (9) Stephen's trial and speech, and death. From this brief but rather thorough list, one can understand the claim that Luke is highly selective in what he is presenting to Theophilus, that Luke has his own norm and purpose in story-telling; a complete history of the Jerusalem enterprise is *not* his goal. He tells us what he wants us to know; his purpose determines all.

8 And Saul was consenting to his death. And on that day a great persecution arose against the church in Jerusalem; and they were all scattered throughout the region of Judea and Samaria, except the apostles. ²Devout men buried Stephen, and made great lamentation over him. ³But Saul was ravaging the church, and entering house after house, he dragged off men and women and committed them to prison.

4 Now those who were scattered went about preaching the word. ⁵Philip went down to a city of Samaria, and proclaimed to them the Christ. ⁶And the multitudes with one accord gave heed to what was said by Philip, when they heard him and saw the signs which he did. ⁷For unclean spirits came out of many who were possessed, crying with a loud voice; and many who were paralyzed or lame were healed. ⁸So there was much joy in that city.

9 But there was a man named Simon who had previously practiced magic in the city and amazed the nation of Samaria, saying that he himself was somebody great. ¹⁰They all gave heed to him, from the least to the greatest, saying, "This man is that power of God which is called Great." ¹¹And they gave heed to him, because for a long time he had amazed them with his magic. ¹²But when they believed Philip as he preached good news about the kingdom of God and the name of Jesus Christ, they were baptized, both men and women. ¹³Even Simon himself believed, and after being baptized he continued with Philip. And seeing signs and great miracles performed, he was amazed.

14 Now when the apostles at Jerusalem heard that Samaria had received the word of God, they sent to them Peter and John, [15]who came down and prayed for them that they might receive the Holy Spirit; [16]for it had not yet fallen on any of them, but they had only been baptized in the name of the Lord Jesus. [17]Then they laid their hands on them and they received the Holy Spirit. [18]Now when Simon saw that the Spirit was given through the laying on of the apostles' hands, he offered them money, [19]saying, "Give me also this power, that any one on whom I lay my hands may receive the Holy Spirit." [20]But Peter said to him, "Your silver perish with you, because you thought you could obtain the gift of God with money! [21]You have neither part nor lot in this matter, for your heart is not right before God. [22]Repent therefore of this wickedness of yours, and pray to the Lord that, if possible, the intent of your heart may be forgiven you. [23]For I see that you are in the gall of bitterness and in the bond of iniquity." [24]And Simon answered, "Pray for me to the Lord, that nothing of what you have said may come upon me."

25 Now when they had testified and spoken the word of the Lord, they returned to Jerusalem, preaching the gospel to many villages of the Samaritans.

26 But an angel of the Lord said to Philip, "Rise and go toward the south to the road that goes down from Jerusalem to Gaza." This is a desert road. [27]And he rose and went. And behold, an Ethiopian, a eunuch, a minister of Candace, queen of the Ethiopians, in charge of all her treasure, had come to Jerusalem to worship [28]and was returning; seated in his chariot, he was reading the prophet Isaiah. [29]And the Spirit said to Philip, "Go up and join this chariot." [30]So Philip ran to him, and heard him reading Isaiah the prophet, and asked, "Do you under-

stand what you are reading?" [31]And he said, "How can I,
unless some one guides me?" And he invited Philip to
come up and sit with him. [32]Now the passage of the
scripture which he was reading was this:

   "As a sheep led to the slaughter
   or a lamb before its shearer is dumb,
   so he opens not his mouth.
  [33]In his humiliation justice was denied him.
   Who can describe his generation?
   For his life is taken up from the earth."

[34]And the eunuch said to Philip, "About whom, pray, does
the prophet say this, about himself or about some one
else?" [35]Then Philip opened his mouth, and beginning
with this scripture he told him the good news of Jesus.
[36]And as they went along the road they came to some
water, and the eunuch said, "See, here is water! What is
to prevent my being baptized?" [38]And he commanded the
chariot to stop, and they both went down into the water,
Philip and the eunuch, and he baptized him. [39]And when
they came up out of the water, the Spirit of the Lord
caught up Philip; and the eunuch saw him no more, and
went on his way rejoicing. [40]But Philip was found at
Azotus, and passing on he preached the gospel to all the
towns till he came to Caesarea.

In the same vein, the persecution against the Hellenist Christians is described in only a few details. Those persecuted went outside Jerusalem into Judea and Samaria (thus, recalling the words of Jesus: "You will be my witnesses in . . . Judea and Samaria"); Saul, the coat-holder, now becomes a major persecutor of the Christians (which prepares for the circumstances we will find him in soon, and for the astounding reversal of his life).

Those who fled the persecution preached; it is needless to underline the fact that these preachers are the Hellenists, not the Palestinian eye-witnesses who were not persecuted.

One of these Hellenist Christians is the second-named in the list of those seven who succeeded the Twelve in service of the widows of Jerusalem. This Philip, who preaches without our having been told that he is authorized to preach, brings the good news learned at the feet of the eye-witness apostles to a town in Samaria, that third of Israel which is between Galilee (on the north) and Judea (on the south). This is the Samaria which claimed that its faithful devotees of Yahweh were the only true children of Abraham and Moses, that the Jews were really blasphemers and not the people of God; even today, though the Samaritans number only about six hundred people, they claim that they are the true followers of Moses, worshiping Yahweh on Mount Ebal in Samaria and waiting for their version of a Messiah, called by them "the Restorer."

Miracles played a major part in the conversion of these Samaritans, as Luke tells us. It seems that wonder-working and magic had a great influence on the Samaritans, for a certain magician (magus), Simon, had earlier won over to his following (and support) these very Samaritans by his powers: they identified him as "Great," a name given to a certain deity of the time. The Samaritans and Simon, the embodiment of the deity, turn to belief in Jesus as the Messiah, the one bringing the kingdom of God to human beings. Whatever the details were of the encounters between Philip and the Samaritans, especially as to how he presented Jesus to them, is not given to us; it is, however, made clear that they ended up believing what the Christians of Jerusalem believed; there is no difference between what the Twelve preached and what the Hellenist Christians preached, as the results show.

Peter and John are sent from Jerusalem to Samaria. Why? Probably to authenticate that the preaching of Philip and its results did indeed conform to the Christian experience with Jesus and in Jerusalem after his departure. As a sign of this unity between Samaria and Jerusalem, it falls to Peter and John to bring down the Spirit upon those baptized by Philip; thus, the two elements of union with Jesus are shaped by the two churches, and reflects the approval of the eye-witnesses on what had happened in Samaria.

One might have suspected that the Spirit would have come upon the Samaritans at their baptism as an integral part of their baptism. Since Luke never talks about the gift of the Spirit which we, through Paul and John, know to be part and parcel of baptism, we must presume that Luke here is speaking about another aspect of the Spirit's entrance into the Christian's life, that aspect which results in the Christian's "prophesying," or "speaking on behalf of God." This is the feature of the Spirit which we saw associated with the baptism of the disciples at Pentecost.

Simon, who had always been agog at the miracles worked by Philip, is now overwhelmed by the coming of the Spirit through the laying on of hands. (It is probably the "prophesying" that draws Simon to this wonder and makes him want to be able to bring down the Spirit himself.) He wants to be able to mediate the Spirit, as had Peter and John; to this end, he is willing to pay money. The response of Peter to this attempt to buy power over the Spirit (this is the first instance of "simony") is swift and fearsome; the language used reminds one of the words of Old Testament prophets as they cajoled and threatened those responsible for terrible offenses against God. As in the case of Ananias and Sapphira, the sin is so evil that the story told to underline its evil allows one to dress Peter and Simon in unusual colors. Simon's response is the proper one to be expected from such a story so in line with biblical thinking: fear, unworthiness to speak to the Lord, request for intercession on behalf of the unworthy one. What happened after Simon's words to Peter is rather immaterial. Luke only wants to highlight the sin, its deserved punishment, and the sinner's proper response.

Peter and John have thus, in their visit to Samaria, given witness and spoken the word the Lord would have them speak; in this they are faithful to the mandate given them by Jesus. Their return to Jerusalem is likewise characterized by this witnessing and preaching.

Philip, on the other hand, is to set off on a road which leads to Gaza, southwest of Jerusalem; note that he is brought into the eventual encounter with the eunuch by a divine directive—for it is God who insists that his word be offered throughout the world. Philip notes, on this road, a certain eunuch; he catches up with his slow-moving chariot and hears the eunuch completing a reading of Isaiah (people often read aloud to themselves these days). The story is neatly arranged in three stages: (1) How can one understand the true meaning of Scripture unless one has an interpreter who truly understands it? (2) About whom is Isaiah speaking in what has become the famous "suffering servant" passage, wherein a silent, humiliated and undefended person, whose life is being cut short and thus will apparently result in no offspring, goes to his death? (3) What else is there, besides repentance and faith (which the eunuch is presupposed to possess), to keep the eunuch from being baptized? In this format, Luke establishes the link between a major Old Testament text and Jesus; the emphasis of the story lies in this— that one will seek baptism only if he can see the relationship between the Old Testament and Jesus.

As with so many other stories, so with this one; the story is brought to a quick finish, once the point is made. The eunuch goes his way to serve the queen of Ethiopia; he goes rejoicing in his being saved. Philip, again under God's direction, evangelizes the western shore of Israel, Judea and Samaria, but we follow him no more.

9

Christ Calls Saul, Who Then Preaches in Damascus and in Jerusalem • Peter Works Cures in Lydia and Jaffa

According to the outline Luke gives us in Acts 1:8 ("... my witnesses ... in Judea and Samaria ..."), we should continue to hear of the witnessing of Philip or of another of the Christians as they pass out of Jerusalem into the territories nearby. However, we meet again a Lucan characteristic to which we become accustomed: Luke often plants a seed which will come to fruition only at the time he has planned in his story-telling; indeed, the presentation now is done as a type of anticipation of and preparation for what is to come. In this case, the witnessing in Judea and Samaria is interrupted by a second and lengthy report about Saul, a report which is meant to be a major form of preparation for Saul's role, from Acts 13 on, as "my witness to the ends of the earth."

The picture of Saul here continues the earlier one of the Saul who approved the killing of Stephen and set about arresting Hellenist Christians right out of their houses. At this moment his enthusiasm to correct these wayward Jews makes him ask the high priest in Jerusalem for letters of introduction which will allow him to comb the synagogues of the great city of Damascus (northeast of and not far from Israel); Saul's purpose is to round up and bring back to Israel and to their senses those Hellenist Jews who have become Christian (some of whom, no doubt, are preaching in Da-

9 But Saul, still breathing threats and murder against the disciples of the Lord, went to the high priest ²and asked him for letters to the synagogues at Damascus, so that if he found any belonging to the Way, men or women, he might bring them bound to Jerusalem. ³Now as he journeyed he approached Damascus, and suddenly a light from heaven flashed about him. ⁴And he fell to the ground and heard a voice saying to him, "Saul, Saul, why do you persecute me?" ⁵And he said, "Who are you, Lord?" And he said, "I am Jesus, whom you are persecuting; ⁶but rise and enter the city, and you will be told what you are to do." ⁷The men who were traveling with him stood speechless, hearing the voice but seeing no one. ⁸Saul arose from the ground; and when his eyes were opened, he could see nothing; so they led him by the hand and brought him into Damascus. ⁹And for three days he was without sight, and neither ate nor drank.

10 Now there was a disciple at Damascus named Ananias. The Lord said to him in a vision, "Ananias." And he said, "Here I am, Lord." ¹¹And the Lord said to him, "Rise and go to the street called Straight, and inquire in the house of Judas for a man of Tarsus named Saul; for behold, he is praying, ¹²and he has seen a man named Ananias come in and lay his hands on him so that he might regain his sight." ¹³But Ananias answered, "Lord, I have heard from many about this man, how much evil he has done to thy saints at Jerusalem; ¹⁴and here he has authority from the chief priests to bind all who call upon thy name." ¹⁵But the Lord said to him, "Go, for he is a chosen instrument of mine to carry my name before the

Gentiles and kings and the sons of Israel; ¹⁶for I will show him how much he must suffer for the sake of my name." ¹⁷So Ananias departed and entered the house. And laying his hands on him he said, "Brother Saul, the Lord Jesus who appeared to you on the road by which you came, has sent me that you may regain your sight and be filled with the Holy Spirit." ¹⁸And immediately something like scales fell from his eyes and he regained his sight. Then he rose and was baptized, ¹⁹and took food and was strengthened.

For several days he was with the disciples at Damascus. ²⁰And in the synagogues immediately he proclaimed Jesus, saying, "He is the Son of God." ²¹And all who heard him were amazed, and said, "Is not this the man who made havoc in Jerusalem of those who called on this name? And he has come here for this purpose, to bring them bound before the chief priests." ²²But Saul increased all the more in strength, and confounded the Jews who lived in Damascus by proving that Jesus was the Christ.

23 When many days had passed, the Jews plotted to kill him, ²⁴but their plot became known to Saul. They were watching the gates day and night, to kill him; ²⁵but his disciples took him by night and let him down over the wall, lowering him in a basket.

26 And when he had come to Jerusalem he attempted to join the disciples; and they were all afraid of him, for they did not believe that he was a disciple. ²⁷But Barnabas took him, and brought him to the apostles, and declared to them how on the road he had seen the Lord, who spoke to him, and how at Damascus he had preached boldly in the name of Jesus. ²⁸So he went in and out among them at Jerusalem, ²⁹preaching boldly in the name of the Lord. And he spoke and disputed against the

Hellenists; but they were seeking to kill him. [30]And when the brethren knew it, they brought him down to Caesarea, and sent him off to Tarsus.

31 So the church throughout all Judea and Galilee and Samaria had peace and was built up; and walking in the fear of the Lord and in the comfort of the Holy Spirit it was multiplied.

32 Now as Peter went here and there among them all, he came down also to the saints that lived at Lydda. [33]There he found a man named Aeneas, who had been bedridden for eight years and was paralyzed. [34]And Peter said to him, "Aeneas, Jesus Christ heals you; rise and make your bed." And immediately he rose. [35]And all the residents of Lydda and Sharon saw him, and they turned to the Lord.

36 Now there was at Joppa a disciple named Tabitha, which means Dorcas. She was full of good works and acts of charity. [37]In those days she fell sick and died; and when they had washed her, they laid her in an upper room. [38]Since Lydda was near Joppa, the disciples, hearing that Peter was there, sent two men to him entreating him, "Please come to us without delay." [39]So Peter rose and went with them. And when he had come, they took him to the upper room. All the widows stood beside him weeping, and showing tunics and other garments which Dorcas made while she was with them. [40]But Peter put them all outside and knelt down and prayed; then turning to the body he said, "Tabitha, rise." And she opened her eyes, and when she saw Peter she sat up. [41]And he gave her his hand and lifted her up. Then calling the saints and widows he presented her alive. [42]And it became known throughout all Joppa, and many believed in the Lord. [43]And he stayed in Joppa for many days with one Simon, a tanner.

mascus, like Philip in Samaria). It is on the road to Damascus that Saul meets his Lord.

What happened to Saul on the way to Damascus can be truly described as his time of conversion; but there is enough to the story Luke tells to see here an interest in looking ahead to Saul's role in the plan of God. Thus, many will refer to this episode as the conversion/mandate story concerning Saul.

Certain facets of the way Luke tells his story are important to note. First, the sudden change from Saul, the aggressor, to Saul, helpless and passive and confused, is not unintentional. As with all other major changes in the story Luke is telling, so here the active role belongs to God and/or his representative(s). From this story no one can have the least doubt as to the real cause of Saul's radical change, nor as to the source of Saul's missionary life on behalf of Jesus. Second, though it is to be assumed, there is no mention of Saul's need for those steps which usually precede the outpouring of the Spirit: repentance and baptism for the forgiveness of sins. Perhaps it is Luke's insistence on these aspects of Christian conversion in the past that allows him to leave them unmentioned now? Third, it is Jesus who is the divine element at the heart of the story, and not, for instance, the Holy Spirit or the angel of the Lord. When it comes to appointing witnesses and making precise the roles they will play, it is Jesus alone who acts; the individual movements of these witnesses are then left to the inspiration of the Spirit or direction of the Lord's angel. Since Acts is, upon reflection, divisible into two major parts, the witness of Peter (and others, in subordinate or momentary roles) and the witness of Paul, it is clear how fundamental to the spread of God's word is the activity and intervention of Jesus from the right hand of the Father. Fourth, the understanding of what role Saul will play is, in this version of the Damascus story, given to the reader through the interplay of the Lord and Ananias; Saul is left in the dark.

The words of Jesus to Ananias are very important for two reasons. First, they are clearly meant to indicate that Saul, hardly a companion of Jesus and not an eye-witness or even a witness who has learned from the eye-witnesses, is nonetheless no less an authorized witness to Jesus than any of the other Christians. There can be no doubt that Saul is the personal choice of Jesus, and this should dispel any doubts as to Saul's authenticity or veracity, no matter what his earlier life had been. Second, Saul will not only bring Jesus' name before Jew and Gentile, high and low (this verse reminds one of the declaration of Jesus in Acts 1:8: witnessing to all); Saul will also learn (from instructions still to be given personally by Jesus) how much he will suffer for Jesus' name.

Once Saul has docilely passed his time of recovery in Damascus, he is quickly presented by Luke as teaching that "Jesus is the Son of God" in the various synagogues of Damascus; indeed, his demonstrations (from Scripture) that Jesus is the Messiah of Israel stunned and confounded Jewish listeners. It should be noted that Luke suggests no "schooling" at the feet of Christians by which he has become a dominating witness to Jesus; Saul's learning came from Jesus himself. Only after some time did certain Jews decide they had had enough of this Saul; their attempts to kill him cause him to leave Damascus and its desert environs and to seek refuge in the hub of Christian communities, the community of Jerusalem. Fear of Saul, experienced earlier as a menace to Christians, makes Christians wary of him; it falls to Barnabas, whose good and trustworthy character we have already been told of, to smooth the way for Saul. In Jerusalem, as in Damascus earlier, Saul is a fearless preacher of the truth he has already come to understand: Jesus is Lord; for this he needed no teaching from the Jerusalem community. But as Stephen, Philip and other Hellenist Christians had experienced in prior years, so now the Hellenist Saul (indeed, being from Tarsus, Saul was not a native-born Jew of Palestine) was unacceptable to the Hellenist Jews of Jerusalem; whatever the native-born Jews thought of Saul, the Hellenist Jews sought to kill him. Saul's escape takes him back through Caesarea-by-the-sea all the way to his home in Tarsus; it is from there that he will enter Acts later.

With this pause in the story of Saul, Luke turns an eye to the summation of Christian witness thus far; there are, he records, churches in all of Israel—Judea, Galilee and Samaria. These churches are in peace, worshiping the Lord (God or Jesus?), and absolutely consoled by God's Spirit.

The witness to Jesus, however, is not altogether completed in Judea and Samaria. We are still to see activities of Peter outside Jerusalem; not only this, but we are to see him play an extremely important part in a story which Luke thinks of immense significance for the understanding of God's mind and will.

To reintroduce Peter and to recall his intimate sharing in the power of Jesus, Luke presents us with two "signs and wonders" which set the stage for Peter's encounter with Cornelius. Peter is journeying northwest of Jerusalem, toward the Mediterranean Sea. He stops many places as he visits Christian groups, and comes to the saints (a title for Christians we are accustomed to hear from Paul's letters) in Lydda. The brevity of the story Luke now tells only adds to underline the major point of the story: "Jesus Christ cures you." Jesus, alive and active, continues his role of Savior from all that domination which human beings cannot rid themselves of. In the second story, which brings Peter to the seashore in Jaffa, the power of Jesus through Peter extends even to giving back life. Who cannot help but remember, as

Peter gives his command to Tabitha, the very similar command of Jesus, on another occasion, to a little girl who had
died (Lk 8:54)? Luke hopes that his reader will remember
and be more convinced that Jesus is active, even though
physically absent. Peter's dependence on Jesus is shown, in
this story, by Peter's need to pray (as Jesus had prayed)
before calling the lady to life. And the effect of the miracles
at Lydda and Jaffa? They are in service of the faith; through
them the people sense the presence of the kingdom of God
through the living Jesus. It is the same living Jesus with
whom we began this chapter, who met Saul on the road; so
alive and a part of the Christian life is he that he can say:
Saul, you are persecuting me!

10

Peter Meets Cornelius and Learns a Major Lesson

Luke has one more story to tell about the "witnessing in Judea and Samaria." This story has to do with Peter, whom we last saw in Jaffa (on the western seaboard of Israel), and Cornelius, a Roman centurion in charge of a hundred Roman soldiers and stationed in Caesarea (about thirty miles up the coast from Jaffa, about fifty-five miles northwest of Jerusalem), a city where most Roman authorities and military lived most of the year, to avoid conflict with the strict Jews in Jerusalem.

The very length of the Cornelius episode suggests that what Luke is recounting here is of immense importance; the episode covers an entire chapter of Acts. One reason for its importance lies in the fact that what emerges from the Cornelius experience will play a major role in a crucial decision for the Christian Church in Acts 15; it was Luke's decision to work out here the lesson Peter learned in this conversion and thus only represent it briefly but convincingly in chapter 15. But even apart from its influence in the later chapter the Cornelius event is most important. Let us turn to its importance now.

The essence of the Cornelius experience, the lesson Peter learned, is made explicit only in chapter 15. In his speech there, Peter notes that God purified the hearts of Cornelius and his household by faith (v 9). This purification is integral to belief in Jesus, implying that to accept Jesus as Lord of one's life and as one's Savior includes repentance

SCRIPTURE TEXT

10At Caesarea there was a man named Cornelius, a centurion of what was known as the Italian Cohort, ²a devout man who feared God with all his household, gave alms liberally to the people, and prayed constantly to God. ³About the ninth hour of the day he saw clearly in a vision an angel of God coming in and saying to him, "Cornelius." ⁴And he stared at him in terror, and said, "What is it, Lord?" And he said to him, "Your prayers and your alms have ascended as a memorial before God. ⁵And now send men to Joppa, and bring one Simon who is called Peter; ⁶he is lodging with Simon, a tanner, whose house is by the seaside." ⁷When the angel who spoke to him had departed, he called two of his servants and a devout soldier from among those that waited on him, ⁸and having related everything to them, he sent them to Joppa.

9 The next day, as they were on their journey and coming near the city, Peter went up on the housetop to pray, about the sixth hour. ¹⁰And he became hungry and desired something to eat; but while they were preparing it, he fell into a trance ¹¹and saw the heaven opened, and something descending, like a great sheet, let down by four corners upon the earth. ¹²In it were all kinds of animals and reptiles and birds of the air. ¹³And there came a voice to him, "Rise, Peter; kill and eat." ¹⁴But Peter said, "No, Lord; for I have never eaten anything that is common or unclean." ¹⁵And the voice came to him again a second time, "What God has cleansed, you must not call common." ¹⁶This happened three times, and the thing was taken up at once to heaven.

17 Now while Peter was inwardly perplexed as to what the vision which he had seen might mean, behold, the men that were sent by Cornelius, having made inquiry for Simon's house, stood before the gate [18]and called out to ask whether Simon who was called Peter was lodging there. [19]And while Peter was pondering the vision, the Spirit said to him, "Behold, three men are looking for you. [20]Rise and go down, and accompany them without hesitation; for I have sent them." [21]And Peter went down to the men and said, "I am the one you are looking for; what is the reason for your coming?" [22]And they said, "Cornelius, a centurion, an upright and God-fearing man, who is well spoken of by the whole Jewish nation, was directed by a holy angel to send for you to come to his house, and to hear what you have to say." [23]So he called them in to be his guests.

The next day he rose and went off with them, and some of the brethren from Joppa accompanied him. [24]And on the following day they entered Caesarea. Cornelius was expecting them and had called together his kinsmen and close friends. [25]When Peter entered, Cornelius met him and fell down at his feet and worshiped him. [26]But Peter lifted him up, saying, "Stand up; I too am a man." [27]And as he talked with him, he went in and found many persons gathered; [28]and he said to them, "You yourselves know how unlawful it is for a Jew to associate with or to visit any one of another nation; but God has shown me that I should not call any man common or unclean. [29]So when I was sent for, I came without objection. I ask then why you sent for me."

30 And Cornelius said, "Four days ago, about this hour, I was keeping the ninth hour of prayer in my house; and behold, a man stood before me in bright apparel, [31]saying, 'Cornelius, your prayer has been heard and your

alms have been remembered before God. [32]Send therefore to Joppa and ask for Simon who is called Peter; he
is lodging in the house of Simon, a tanner, by the seaside.'
[33]So I sent to you at once, and you have been kind enough
to come. Now therefore we are all here present in the
sight of God, to hear all that you have been commanded
by the Lord."

34 And Peter opened his mouth and said: "Truly I
perceive that God shows no partiality, [35]but in every
nation any one who fears him and does what is right is
acceptable to him. [36]You know the word which he sent
to Israel, preaching good news of peace by Jesus Christ
(he is Lord of all), [37]the word which was proclaimed
throughout all Judea, beginning from Galilee after the
baptism which John preached: [38]how God anointed Jesus
of Nazareth with the Holy Spirit and with power; how he
went about doing good and healing all that were oppressed by the devil, for God was with him. [39]And we are
witnesses to all that he did both in the country of the
Jews and in Jerusalem. They put him to death by hanging
him on a tree; [40]but God raised him on the third day and
made him manifest; [41]not to all the people but to us who
were chosen by God as witnesses, who ate and drank
with him after he rose from the dead. [42]And he commanded us to preach to the people, and to testify that he is the
one ordained by God to be judge of the living and the
dead. [43]To him all the prophets bear witness that every
one who believes in him receives forgiveness of sins
through his name."

44 While Peter was still saying this, the Holy Spirit
fell on all who heard the word. [45]And the believers from
among the circumcised who came with Peter were
amazed, because the gift of the Holy Spirit had been
poured out even on the Gentiles. [46]For they heard them

speaking in tongues and extolling God. Then Peter declared, [47]"Can any one forbid water for baptizing these people who have received the Holy Spirit just as we have?" [48]And he commanded them to be baptized in the name of Jesus Christ. Then they asked him to remain for some days.

for one's former life and a commitment to a new way of life according to Jesus' teaching. Thus, faith includes a new way of living, as well as a new source of salvation.

That Peter learns of this fundamental act of faith is conveyed in a novel way. As the story is told to us, Cornelius and his household are not described as "believers," as people "repentant and asking for baptism in the name of Jesus," as Acts 2:38 would lead us to expect. All that is said is that, quite unexpected by Peter, the Holy Spirit is poured out on Cornelius and his household, even to their reproducing the gifts of the Spirit which the disciples enjoyed on Pentecost. That Peter moves from this witness of outpouring to offering baptism to Cornelius implies that Cornelius and his household have passed through the moment of repentance which leads to baptism and are ready for baptism itself. Indeed, the presence of the Spirit, usually reserved as the culmination of baptism, here follows upon the interior moment of acceptance of Jesus (about whom Peter is in the act of presenting). Luke presents the Spirit earlier than usual for a purpose which we will consider in a moment. What is important here is that one realize that Luke, without making it explicit, teaches that faith given by God cleanses as well as unites to Jesus. It is not Cornelius' earlier life of piety, then, which made him clean for baptism; it was the faith given him by God that made him so. To this faith comes God's greatest gift: the Spirit.

But there is more to the story of Cornelius than his moment of belief, the moment of Peter's understanding at the outpouring of the Spirit. Why is there more? Well, there is another very important and related lesson to be learned from the full story. The teaching we just described concerning faith as cleansing certainly argues that Cornelius can be baptized; he already has the effect of baptism. But implicit to the reception of such faith is the preaching, a preaching which brings Jewish Christians into contact with Gentiles. That Jews (even Christians) should enjoy the widest contact with Gentiles implies a degree of intimacy which Jewish traditions by and large forbade. Specifically forbidden were entry into a Gentile's house and eating with Gentiles. Therefore, integral to the lesson Peter learns about the cleansing involved in belief in Jesus is the understanding that he, and others, can indeed mix with Gentiles to bring them the good news of God's salvation, without the restrictions imposed by Jewish tradition. But this understanding meant a change of mind, and this meant that God had to enlighten Peter (and through him the rest of the Church) so that he could learn the truth, God's truth, about the Gentiles. This truth is played out in a vision, but it can be summed up in the words of God within the vision: "What I have declared clean you shall no longer consider unclean."

"Uncleanness," "impurity," was considered to be the normal, expected state of the Gentile, for he had no knowledge of the true God and thus wandered in idol-worship and wallowed in a life which reflected idol-worship. To come into more intimate contact with a Gentile was to defile oneself, the Jews thought, and this defilement required a formal rite to turn one back to a state in which one can stand before God worthily. It is to realize something which for centuries had not been known—that there is need of vision, words of the Lord, guidance of the Holy Spirit. Indeed, the reader is even made aware of the good life of Cornelius, as a sign to him (though not to Peter) that the Gentile is not unclean, as supposed.

Peter, then, is to learn two lessons, that faith cleanses and that living intimately with Gentiles is in accord with God's will.

There are two other aspects of the Cornelius story which call for our attention. Here, as much as anywhere else

in the Gospel or Acts, the story is told in such a way that
the two main characters are essentially passive. All that gives
movement to the story comes from above, from God. This
dependence of Peter and Cornelius on the divine pleasure
for each step each one takes is really a theological statement:
it is God who intervened drastically to bring about the manner of Jewish Christian preaching to Gentiles and the willingness of Jewish Christians to baptize Gentiles. Implicit in
all this is the understanding that without such a help from
God for the Jewish Christians, both baptism of Gentiles and
bringing the preaching to them would have been seriously
hindered, if not impossible.

Moreover, once Cornelius asks Peter to speak "whatever
directives the Lord has given you," Cornelius recedes and
Peter stands front and center. Why is this? Because ultimately the Cornelius episode is not so much a story of a
wonderful conversion to Christianity as it is a moment of
crucial insight for those who are already disciples of Jesus
and who must witness to Jesus "to the ends of the earth."
In other words, the lesson Peter learned here is every bit
as important to the carrying out of the Book of Acts as the
announcement that Cornelius has become a Christian.

One should note with interest how Peter presents the
saving message of God to Cornelius. To make the point from
a grammatical approach, practically every main verb of the
speech has God, not Jesus, as its subject. This is a concrete
way of Luke to express the fact that the God whom Cornelius worships and serves is the God who has brought Jesus
to be Savior; thus, the Jesus event is integrated into Cornelius' active religious life, and made to be seen as a flow-
ering of the will of that God whom Cornelius loves to obey.
What might be a significant stumbling block for Cornelius—
that is, the death of Jesus—is removed by the insistence that

Jesus was raised up by Cornelius' God, and thus can be taken as one's Lord.

Cornelius had tried to live a life pleasing to God. He learns now that forgiveness for what has displeased God can be his, but it must come through union with Jesus, through baptism. Peter understood that he was to witness to Jesus to the ends of the earth. He learns now lessons he never caught sight of before: that the Gentiles' faith implies a cleansing of their sins and that the Gentiles are not to be considered anymore as "unclean." Each major character, and the reader, too, has learned from God how God looks at the reality in things. Now Peter must convince his fellow Christians in Jerusalem.

11

Peter Explains Himself to the Jewish Christians of Jerusalem • We Hear of Antioch in Syria and of Its Charity to Jerusalem

We begin a new chapter, but we continue with the story of Peter and Cornelius, for it is a most important story to Acts and to the Church. Peter has been convinced, as have his traveling companions, of certain truths, but it is obvious that these lessons were not to be learned only by the chief eye-witness and his companions in Jaffa. These truths are such that the whole Church must learn them and embrace them wholeheartedly. Everyone is asked to undergo a change of mind.

Peter's speech is noteworthy for its fidelity to all that Luke had earlier reported about the Cornelius episode. Indeed, over half the speech is taken word-for-word from the account given in chapter 10. In this way, the reader is able to assure all that what Peter reports to his fellow Christians is an authentic witness of God's interventions. If anything, the speech emphasizes even more than the earlier narrative the divine element in the experience of Peter.

It is true that nothing in this speech is reported of the preaching about Jesus which Cornelius heard. But the point at stake now is not to what kind of preaching Cornelius responded, but on what grounds Peter presumed to break with Jewish traditions regarding Gentile uncleanness and to baptize people defined publicly as impure, unclean, unrepentant. Luke has tailored his story-telling to the circumstances, as usual.

SCRIPTURE TEXT

11 Now the apostles and the brethren who were in Judea heard that the Gentiles also had received the word of God. ²So when Peter went up to Jerusalem, the circumcision party criticized him, ³saying, "Why did you go to uncircumcised men and eat with them?" ⁴But Peter began and explained to them in order: ⁵"I was in the city of Joppa praying; and in a trance I saw a vision, something descending, like a great sheet, let down from heaven by four corners; and it came down to me. ⁶Looking at it closely I observed animals and beasts of prey and reptiles and birds of the air. ⁷And I heard a voice saying to me, 'Rise, Peter; kill and eat.' ⁸But I said, 'No, Lord; for nothing common or unclean has ever entered my mouth.' ⁹But the voice answered a second time from heaven, 'What God has cleansed you must not call common.' ¹⁰This happened three times, and all was drawn up again into heaven. ¹¹At that very moment three men arrived at the house in which we were, sent to me from Caesarea. ¹²And the Spirit told me to go with them, making no distinction. These six brethren also accompanied me, and we entered the man's house. ¹³And he told us how he had seen the angel standing in his house and saying, 'Send to Joppa and bring Simon called Peter; ¹⁴he will declare to you a message by which you will be saved, you and all your household.' ¹⁵As I began to speak, the Holy Spirit fell on them just as on us at the beginning. ¹⁶And I remembered the word of the Lord, how he said, 'John baptized with water, but you shall be baptized with the Holy Spirit.' ¹⁷If then God gave the same gift to them as he gave to us when we believed in the Lord Jesus

Christ, who was I that I could withstand God?" [18]When they heard this they were silenced. And they glorified God, saying, "Then to the Gentiles also God has granted repentance unto life."

19 Now those who were scattered because of the persecution that arose over Stephen traveled as far as Phoenicia and Cyprus and Antioch, speaking the word to none except Jews. [20]But there were some of them, men of Cyprus and Cyrene, who on coming to Antioch spoke to the Greeks also, preaching the Lord Jesus. [21]And the hand of the Lord was with them, and a great number that believed turned to the Lord. [22]News of this came to the ears of the church in Jerusalem, and they sent Barnabas to Antioch. [23]When he came and saw the grace of God, he was glad; and he exhorted them all to remain faithful to the Lord with steadfast purpose; [24]for he was a good man, full of the Holy Spirit and of faith. And a large company was added to the Lord. [25]So Barnabas went to Tarsus to look for Saul; [26]and when he had found him, he brought him to Antioch. For a whole year they met with the church, and taught a large company of people; and in Antioch the disciples were for the first time called Christians.

27 Now in these days prophets came down from Jerusalem to Antioch. [28]And one of them named Agabus stood up and foretold by the Spirit that there would be a great famine over all the world; and this took place in the days of Claudius. [29]And the disciples determined, every one according to his ability, to send relief to the brethren who lived in Judea; [30]and they did so, sending it to the elders by the hand of Barnabas and Saul.

The Cornelius episode comes to a complete end now with the approval of what Peter did. This approval is expressed in a striking form: the Gentiles have been given by God the repentance which leads to life. One can see in this formulation how Jewish Christians have made sense of the Gentiles' experience and used their traditional vocabulary to express their understanding. They understand, in short, that Cornelius has repented, though Peter later will prefer to say that God cleansed the Gentiles' hearts through the kind of faith he gave them. This is the central lesson Luke teaches at this time, though one is not to lose sight of the fact that the Jerusalem Church has a new understanding regarding eating and visiting with Gentiles. With the teaching completed regarding Cornelius, the Jewish Christian Church is now able to handle the imminent conversion of many, many Gentiles with peace and joy. That they were allowed to come this far in their experience of Jesus and God without these basic understandings is mysterious and a witness to the development of human understanding about God, even after the public life of Jesus is over. They are now ready to greet the new efforts directed to Gentiles the world over; ironically it is not they but the Hellenist Jewish Christians who will actually contact the Gentiles. The lessons, however, belong to the entire Church; Luke wants this understood.

It is only after the Cornelius story that Luke tells his readers about the Hellenist Jewish Christians who went beyond Judea and Samaria, to Phoenicia (Lebanon today is part of this), to the island of Cyprus, and to Antioch, a famous city of Paul's day which is found today on the border between Syria and the southeastern corner of Turkey. These Christians, Luke tells us, spoke not only to Jews, but to Greeks (i.e., Gentiles and pagans). When Luke tells us that these Christians were part of the group that had to flee Jerusalem at the time of Stephen's death, one might ask why

Luke did not tell us about them then (as he did for Philip
in Samaria and Peter in Judea), for they belong to that immediate post-Stephen time. We now perceive this reason.
Luke wanted the lessons learned in the Cornelius episode
to be well understood; then he would introduce us to the
efforts of Christians among the Gentiles of Antioch in Syria.
The way Luke used the Cornelius story as a theological
preparation for events which actually happened before the
Cornelius episode is a good example of how Luke's order
of things need not be in chronological order (as we might
expect), yet is an order which he thinks will best help Theophilus grasp well the reliability of the things he has been
taught. Luke's order, then, in his Gospel and in Acts need
not be chronological.

As with the Samaritan conversions, so with these in Antioch: the Jerusalem Church, the Church of the eye-witnesses, should confirm the fact that what has occurred in
Antioch, what made up the witness to these people, is in
fact a genuinely Christian occurrence, a genuinely Christian
witness. Strangely, the one to decide this is not an eye-witness, but a Hellenist, Barnabas from Cyprus; it is in order to
strengthen Barnabas' authority that Luke here gives a greater
insight than before to Barnabas' trustworthiness in this task.
Barnabas, who had earlier been instrumental in Saul's acceptance in Jerusalem, now brings Saul to Antioch, where they
both, we learn, are qualified as teachers of Christianity. Indeed, it is from here that the Pauline missionary efforts will
begin. It is also here in Antioch that the believers in Jesus
first are called Christians, a name derived from the Greek
language (*Christos*), which, though well known in Israel,
would not have been the language used to describe Jesus'
followers and representatives.

It is not by chance that Luke dwells particularly on the
city of Antioch. Antioch was, next to Rome and Alexandria,

the third greatest city in the Roman Empire. Scholars are willing more and more these days to credit Antioch with being the real source of the missionary efforts which carried Christianity beyond its Jewish lines into the whole world of the time; this is especially argued in the light of the fact that Jerusalem, with members of its community still dissatisfied with the openness to Gentile membership which paid so little, if any attention to the staples of Judaism, was thoroughly destroyed in 70 A.D., and thus lost any Christian dynamism from that original community.

One of the signs of God's pleasure with the Christians was the gift of his Spirit to them, which manifested itself in many ways, not the least of which was in prophecy. It is prophets of Jerusalem who come to Antioch to warn of a famine that would occur before 54 A.D. It is certainly consonant with Luke's earlier emphases, in describing Christian communities, that Antioch shows itself to be true to its Christian roots by sending financial help to the Church in Jerusalem and in Judea. It falls to Barnabas and Saul to deliver these donations from the third greatest city of the Empire.

12

Peter Jailed and Liberated, While His
Oppressor Is Punished • Barnabas and Saul
Reside in Antioch

Loosely associated in a temporal way with the events
Luke has recounted about the new community of Antioch,
the capital of Syria at this time in history, is the arrest and
murder of James. This is the James, one of the Twelve and
an eye-witness to all that occurred from the baptism of Jesus
until his ascension, who was called with his brother John
and with Peter and Andrew to be fishers of men. James'
arch-persecutor is a Herod, the grandson of Herod the Great,
Herod Agrippa I. Herod Agrippa I had spent some time as
a political prisoner in the jails of Rome under Emperor Caligula; a prison companion was Claudius. When Caligula met
his gruesome end, it was Claudius who was named Emperor,
in 41 A.D. Agrippa had been not only a friend of Claudius
in prison, but also a supporter in Claudius' accession to the
power of emperor; as a result, in 41 A.D. Claudius gave to
Agrippa control of the middle and southern thirds of Israel,
and so it came about that it was this Herod, Agrippa I, who
was prominent in the persecution of certain Christians. Since
we know that Agrippa I died in 44 A.D., we follow Luke's
thought in concluding that, with chapter 12, we find ourselves in 45 A.D., about fifteen year's distance from the beginning of Acts.

Agrippa I persecuted not only James; he had Peter arrested in Jerusalem in the hope of pleasing certain Jews by
putting Peter to death. What actually happened to this ty-

SCRIPTURE TEXT

12 About that time Herod the king laid violent hands upon some who belonged to the church. ²He killed James the brother of John with the sword; ³and when he saw that it pleased the Jews, he proceeded to arrest Peter also. This was during the days of Unleavened Bread. ⁴And when he had seized him, he put him in prison, and delivered him to four squads of soldiers to guard him, intending after the Passover to bring him out to the people. ⁵So Peter was kept in prison; but earnest prayer for him was made to God by the church.

6 The very night when Herod was about to bring him out, Peter was sleeping between two soldiers, bound with two chains, and sentries before the door were guarding the prison; ⁷and behold, an angel of the Lord appeared, and a light shone in the cell; and he struck Peter on the side and woke him, saying, "Get up quickly." And the chains fell off his hands. ⁸And the angel said to him, "Dress yourself and put on your sandals." And he did so. And he said to him, "Wrap your mantle around you and follow me." ⁹And he went out and followed him; he did not know that what was done by the angel was real, but thought he was seeing a vision. ¹⁰When they had passed the first and the second guard, they came to the iron gate leading into the city. It opened to them of its own accord, and they went out and passed on through one street; and immediately the angel left him. ¹¹And Peter came to himself, and said, "Now I am sure that the Lord has sent his angel and rescued me from the hand of Herod and from all that the Jewish people were expecting."

12 When he realized this, he went to the house of Mary, the mother of John whose other name was Mark, where many were gathered together and were praying. [13]And when he knocked at the door of the gateway, a maid named Rhoda came to answer. [14]Recognizing Peter's voice, in her joy she did not open the gate but ran in and told that Peter was standing at the gate. [15]They said to her, "You are mad." But she insisted that it was so. They said, "It is his angel!" [16]But Peter continued knocking; and when they opened, they saw him and were amazed. [17]But motioning to them with his hand to be silent, he described to them how the Lord had brought him out of the prison. And he said, "Tell this to James and to the brethren." Then he departed and went to another place.

18 Now when day came, there was no small stir among the soldiers over what had become of Peter. [19]And when Herod had sought for him and could not find him, he examined the sentries and ordered that they should be put to death. Then he went down from Judea to Caesarea, and remained there.

20 Now Herod was angry with the people of Tyre and Sidon; and they came to him in a body, and having persuaded Blastus, the king's chamberlain, they asked for peace, because their country depended on the king's country for food. [21]On an appointed day Herod put on his royal robes, took his seat upon the throne, and made an oration to them. [22]And the people shouted, "The voice of a god, and not of man!" [23]Immediately an angel of the Lord smote him, because he did not give God the glory; and he was eaten by worms and died.

24 But the word of God grew and multiplied.

25 And Barnabas and Saul returned from Jerusalem

when they had fulfilled their mission, bringing with them John whose other name was Mark.

rannical plan is told in story form, and the story is not without its humor. But the point of the story, a point made more
than once in Acts, teaches how futile are the attempts even
of mighty powers like Herod Agrippa I to stifle the preachers
of God's word. Luke often builds his stories on Old Testament story styles, because those were the stories *par excellence* through the medium of which people immediately
recognized the power of God which overcomes all enemies
and saves his chosen ones. These Old Testament forms of
storytelling are constructed to reveal as fully as possible the
divine influence on human events; in search of such a
method of revelation Luke uses this form of story-telling. An
added benefit of reversion to Old Testament-type story-telling is that Peter appears as in direct line of those heroes of
the past for whom God had intervened to save from human
machinations.

     Peter goes free and heads for the house of Mary, the
mother of John Mark; this Mark will be, for a while, a companion of Paul and is, traditionally, the author of Mark's Gospel. Peter's last words should not be missed; he asks Mary's
household to tell of his most recent liberation to "James and
the brothers." Who is this James? This is James, a relative of
Jesus (thus, not one of the Twelve), who had been one of
those present at Jesus' ascension and a part of those days
which preceded it, and one of those upon whom the Spirit
was poured out at Pentecost. We find him later on so presented as to allow us to think of him as the leader of the
Christian Church in Jerusalem, a Church we will see to have
many members who still cannot accept the way in which
other Church members allow the Gentiles to enter into
Christian fellowship. By singling out James at this early point
in Acts, Peter seems to reveal already that James has a role
of leadership in the community, even though he was not
one of the Twelve. It seems, then, that to be one of the

Twelve meant to be one of the foundation stones of Jesus' community; it does not seem to have implied that all Twelve are the actual day-to-day leaders of the community. To the Twelve belongs the pre-eminent role of witness *par excellence* and foundation.

This story gives some explanation for the disappearance of Peter from Jerusalem (i.e., to escape the clutches of Herod) and thus allows Luke to turn from the sphere of influence of Peter, and from the fulfillment of Jesus' will that witness be given in Jerusalem, Judea and Samaria. Luke is now ready to narrate the word of the Lord in its indomitable march to the ends of the earth. But the story also shows how Peter, to the extent that God allowed, imitated his Master under the cruelty and injustice of (another) Herod.

Herod Agrippa I, history itself recalls, died a miserable death in Caesarea-by-the-sea (where non-religious people resided and thus avoided clashes with the religious people of Jerusalem). It is fitting that Christians ascribed their own suffering under Herod as cause for his sad death (Christians often explained historical occurrences in light of their own relationship to the people and places involved in those occurrences). The cause of Herod's death was his refusal to admit that the glory which his lackeys were giving to him belonged only to God; but this pride of Herod was only the continuance of those evil qualities he exhibited in the case of James and Peter. Luke is not averse to spending some time in teaching what becomes of those (e.g., Judas Iscariot, Ananias and Sapphira, Simon Magus) who challenge God. These people are, in their own ways, foreshadowed by and a continuation of all those who, in Old Testament times, severely challenged God.

The word of God continues to spread (presumably Luke has his eye now particularly on the area of Antioch). He brings Barnabas and Saul, with John Mark, back from Jeru-

salem to Antioch, thus preparing his characters for their first
mission of witnessing which must begin from Antioch.

It is obvious that the witnesses to Christ were many
who spread the good news to many areas outside Israel; it
is not these whom Luke will follow in his story of witness
to the ends of the earth. Luke is quite particular about how
he will proceed. We must always remember that his goal is
not an account of the spread of Christianity, but a writing
which will give Theophilus the greatest assurance and confidence as regards those things which he had been taught.
Can one see how these first twelve chapters have contributed to the goal?

13

*The Spirit's Task for Paul and Barnabas • A
Struggle in Cyprus • Preaching in Antioch • A
Turn to the Gentiles and Persecution*

No doubt, from this point on to the end of Acts, we
read of witnessing beyond Israel to the "ends of the earth,"
as Jesus had put it (Acts 1:8). We should realize, however,
that the witnessing we follow is a very specially chosen witnessing, that of St. Paul. In some instances St. Paul is the
founder of a Christian community, but not always. Thus, he
is not presented under the heading of the "beginner of Christian communities"; what is to be attended to is his witness,
a witness, we shall see, which is not simply verbal or oral.

The beginnings of the Church in Antioch were only
very briefly told; no doubt we are to transfer to the Antioch
scene what we have learned from earlier chapters about the
beginnings of Christian life in earlier years. We do know,
however, the essential element of the Antioch community,
whatever might have been the differences between Christians, eye-witnesses and companions of Jesus, in Israel and
those in Antioch: "The good news of the Lord Jesus was
preached to them . . . they believed in and turned to the
Lord . . . and were encouraged to persevere in their commitment to him" (Acts 11:20–23).

Barnabas and Saul (together with John Mark) have been
in Antioch as teachers for some time, as Luke picks up again
interest in them. We find that they are not only teachers
(presumably qualified to continue the teaching of Jesus and
those whom he had taught), but also prophets, those gifted

SCRIPTURE TEXT

13 Now in the church at Antioch there were prophets and teachers, Barnabas, Simeon who was
called Niger, Lucius of Cyrene, Manaen a member of the
court of Herod the tetrarch, and Saul. [2]While they were
worshiping the Lord and fasting, the Holy Spirit said, "Set
apart for me Barnabas and Saul for the work to which I
have called them." [3]Then after fasting and praying they
laid their hands on them and sent them off.

4 So, being sent out by the Holy Spirit, they went
down to Seleucia; and from there they sailed to Cyprus.
[5]When they arrived at Salamis, they proclaimed the word
of God in the synagogues of the Jews. And they had John
to assist them. [6]When they had gone through the whole
island as far as Paphos, they came upon a certain magician, a Jewish false prophet, named Bar-Jesus. [7]He was
with the proconsul, Sergius Paulus, a man of intelligence,
who summoned Barnabas and Saul and sought to hear
the word of God. [8]But Elymas the magician (for that is
the meaning of his name) withstood them, seeking to
turn away the proconsul from the faith. [9]But Saul, who
is also called Paul, filled with the Holy Spirit, looked
intently at him [10]and said, "You son of the devil, you
enemy of all righteousness, full of all deceit and villainy,
will you not stop making crooked the straight paths of
the Lord? [11]And now, behold, the hand of the Lord is
upon you, and you shall be blind and unable to see the
sun for a time." Immediately mist and darkness fell upon
him and he went about seeking people to lead him by the
hand. [12]Then the proconsul believed, when he saw what

had occurred, for he was astonished at the teaching of the Lord.

13 Now Paul and his company set sail from Paphos, and came to Perga in Pamphylia. And John left them and returned to Jerusalem; [14]but they passed on from Perga and came to Antioch of Pisidia. And on the sabbath day they went into the synagogue and sat down. [15]After the reading of the law and the prophets, the rulers of the synagogue sent to them, saying, "Brethren, if you have any word of exhortation for the people, say it." [16]So Paul stood up, and motioning with his hand said:

"Men of Israel, and you that fear God, listen. [17]The God of this people Israel chose our fathers and made the people great during their stay in the land of Egypt, and with uplifted arm he led them out of it. [18]And for about forty years he bore with them in the wilderness. [19]And when he had destroyed seven nations in the land of Canaan, he gave them their land as an inheritance, for about four hundred and fifty years. [20]And after that he gave them judges until Samuel the prophet. [21]Then they asked for a king; and God gave them Saul the son of Kish, a man of the tribe of Benjamin, for forty years. [22]And when he had removed him, he raised up David to be their king; of whom he testified and said, 'I have found in David the son of Jesse a man after my heart, who will do all my will.' [23]Of this man's posterity God has brought to Israel a Savior, Jesus, as he promised. [24]Before his coming John had preached a baptism of repentance to all the people of Israel. [25]And as John was finishing his course, he said, 'What do you suppose that I am? I am not he. No, but after me one is coming, the sandals of whose feet I am not worthy to untie.'

26 "Brethren, sons of the family of Abraham, and those among you that fear God, to us has been sent the

message of this salvation. ²⁷For those who live in Jerusalem and their rulers, because they did not recognize him
nor understand the utterances of the prophets which are
read every sabbath, fulfilled these by condemning him.
²⁸Though they could charge him with nothing deserving
death, yet they asked Pilate to have him killed. ²⁹And
when they had fulfilled all that was written of him, they
took him down from the tree, and laid him in a tomb.
³⁰But God raised him from the dead; ³¹and for many days
he appeared to those who came up with him from Gali-
lee to Jerusalem, who are now his witnesses to the people. ³²And we bring you the good news that what God
promised to the fathers, ³³this he has fulfilled to us their
children by raising Jesus; as also it is written in the
second psalm,

> 'Thou art my Son,
> today I have begotten thee.'

³⁴And as for the fact that he raised him from the dead, no
more to return to corruption, he spoke in this way,

> 'I will give you the holy and sure blessings of
> David.'

³⁵Therefore he says also in another psalm,

> 'Thou wilt not let thy Holy One see corruption.'

³⁶For David, after he had served the counsel of God in his
own generation, fell asleep, and was laid with his fathers,
and saw corruption; ³⁷but he whom God raised up saw
no corruption. ³⁸Let it be known to you therefore, brethren, that through this man forgiveness of sins is proclaimed to you, ³⁹and by him every one that believes is
freed from everything from which you could not be
freed by the law of Moses. ⁴⁰Beware, therefore, lest there
come upon you what is said in the prophets:

> ⁴¹'Behold, you scoffers, and wonder, and perish;
> for I do a deed in your days,

a deed you will never believe, if one declares it
   to you.' "

42 As they went out, the people begged that these
things might be told them the next sabbath. [43]And when
the meeting of the synagogue broke up, many Jews and
devout converts to Judaism followed Paul and Barnabas,
who spoke to them and urged them to continue in the
grace of God.

44 The next sabbath almost the whole city gathered
together to hear the word of God. [45]But when the Jews
saw the multitudes, they were filled with jealousy, and
contradicted what was spoken by Paul, and reviled him.
[46]And Paul and Barnabas spoke out boldly, saying, "It was
necessary that the word of God should be spoken first to
you. Since you thrust it from you, and judge yourselves
unworthy of eternal life, behold, we turn to the Gentiles.
[47]For so the Lord has commanded us, saying,

   'I have set you to be a light for the Gentiles,
   that you may bring salvation to the uttermost
      parts of the earth.' "

48 And when the Gentiles heard this, they were
glad and glorified the word of God; and as many as were
ordained to eternal life believed. [49]And the word of the
Lord spread throughout all the region. [50]But the Jews
incited the devout women of high standing and the leading men of the city, and stirred up persecution against
Paul and Barnabas, and drove them out of their district.
[51]But they shook off the dust from their feet against them,
and went to Iconium. [52]And the disciples were filled with
joy and with the Holy Spirit.

to be able to speak special messages on behalf of God. Now, at a particular worship of God and in a context of fasting, the Spirit indicates the will of God that Barnabas and Saul be put aside for a task to which the Spirit calls them. As with Jesus, so with his disciples, the Spirit moves to preaching, to witnessing. As far as possible, Luke likes to frame divine interventions like this of the Spirit within a religious context; he had done this with Jesus, Zechariah, Mary, Simeon, Peter—now it is done for Barnabas and Saul. The particular work to which the Spirit refers will be completed in chapter 14; it is only one explicitation of that goal and purpose for which Jesus called Saul. The Spirit, then, concretizes the fundamental role Jesus continues to play in the life of his witnesses; recall that it was Jesus who was responsible for the Spirit's presence in the witnessing in Jerusalem. With prayer, fasting and approval Barnabas and Saul move out under the Spirit's impulse.

Antioch, like many great cities, was close to but not right on the Mediterranean Sea. Inland about twenty miles, Antioch rested on a river leading from the sea, but it had great use for an outlet, a town, closer to the sea, and so there grew up Seleucia, the actual port and point of contact of Antioch (on the Orontes River) and the rest of the Mediterranean. Seleucia is found about sixteen miles southwest of Antioch, about five miles north of the sea itself; from here Barnabas, Saul and John Mark depart.

Their first goal was Cyprus, actually the city of Salamis, on Cyprus' eastern shore and one hundred and thirty miles from the Antioch area. Luke restricts himself to a generalized description of the Cyprus evangelizing and to a particular episode which occurs at the other end of the island. The pattern of preaching locations is to be noted; Paul always went first to synagogues, first because he felt that the good news was to be given to Jews first, and second because synagogues were the best places to meet Gentiles already sympathetic to the true God, Gentiles who could lead Paul to others. At the western end of the island Paul met the representative of Rome, the proconsular governor, Sergius Paulus. Whether or not the governor was baptized can be debated, but, as one who was intelligent and approached Christianity with an open mind, he responds properly to the message and the power of Paul. Unfortunately, a certain magician (meant to echo that other magician, Simon, whom Peter met in Samaria), called Bar-Jesus or Elymas, tried to stop Paul; since magicians depended for their livelihood on their ability to keep wealthy people's attention, Elymas saw Paul as a sure threat to his dominion and income. Paul is reminiscent of Old Testament prophets; his anger, vigor, righteousness, and punishing are characteristics which Luke wants here displayed, first, to underline the seriousness of the evil Elymas tries to inflict on God, second, to emphasize the intimate link between Paul and God, and, third, to buttress this first picture of Paul as defender of Christianity and close imitator of Peter. Having presented Paul this way once, Luke never does it again.

Luke quickly takes us to the mainland, to Perga (about one hundred and eighty miles northwest of Paphos on Cyprus), in present-day Turkey. From Perga Luke moves Paul and Barnabas (Mark went home for some unexplained reason) quickly to Antioch, about ninety miles north of Perga. Here Paul gives what must be described as *the* representative proclamation of Christianity to the Judaism which was scattered outside Israel; Luke offers no other speech to this audience.

It is important to understand this speech as an answer to the request made of Paul and Barnabas by the leaders of the synagogue; they ask, as they would of any visitors, for "words of exhortation, encouragement, consolation"—and

Paul's speech is precisely an exhortation which encourages and consoles. It is an exhortation to believe in Jesus. Why believe in Jesus? "It is through him that the forgiveness of sins is proclaimed . . . remission of those penalties that those who disobey the law of Moses deserve" (vv 38–39). The message, then, is ultimately a source of joy, of consolation, for now one knows how one's sins can be forgiven—and forgiveness was a most cherished value. But Paul offers more to his audience than the hope of forgiveness. Paul indicates that what he is offering is grounded in the love God has shown to Israel from the calling of Israel's ancestors, through the protection of Israel in Egypt, the giving to Israel of the land, the care of the judges, the protection of the kings, culminating in the promise made to David that God would provide for Israel a Savior. The Savior appeared in Israel, witnessed to by John the Baptist. All these acts of love were meant to bring this Savior to the Israel of this moment. Yet, Jesus was rejected and put to death.

Death is no sign that Jesus is not the Savior. The Scriptures had foretold it, and, after it happened, God raised Jesus from death's corruption. What David never had was given to Jesus—life eternal, life without corruption. It is because of Jesus' eternal life that Paul can announce that from the moment of Jesus' resurrection there exists forever that Son of David who, God promised, would reign forever and bring peace to Israel forever. Isaiah had promised that God would create a new, eternal covenant for Israel which would bring to Israel the holy mercies assured to David. But for this eternal covenant there had to be the eternal Son of David, and this Son of David, in order to be eternal, had to rise from the dead after his crucifixion. Thus, the Jews should know that the King is now eternal; this means that the kingdom is now underway for those who will only listen. How, indeed, can Jews enter the kingdom now taking shape if they refuse the King through whom they are to receive the mercies of the kingdom?

The fulfillment of the promise is the greatest expression of the love which has moved God from the beginning of Israel's history. But God has also arranged that forgiveness, so necessary an element for entry into the kingdom, will be available to the Jews in a way that they never experienced before. They can now be known as "just," freed from the penalties of sin which could never be wiped away before by the Jewish system. How is it that now, in a new way, the Jews are finally able to be "just," "holy," "worthy to enter the kingdom"? Without explaining very much, Paul outlines this new opportunity: it is "in Jesus" that one who believes can be justified. It seems that Paul is implying here what he explains in great detail in his Letters to the Galatians and Romans, that Jesus' death has made up for our sins and that we will enjoy forgiveness flowing from his death if we believe in him as the one who actually has won our forgiveness by his death.

Paul knows that he has only outlined the case for belief in Jesus; he hastens to remind the Jews about earlier scoffers of God's loving words, in the hope that this reminder will keep the Jews open to further discussions and to faith.

This is Paul's only speech recorded for the Jews of the diaspora. It is only in outline form, though it still provides not only the major kinds of arguments Paul used (interconnecting the events of Jesus' life with the expectations of the Scriptures) but also motives for belief in the person he proposes to them.

As jealousy plagued Jesus, then Peter, so it hounds Paul. This jealousy is given as the reason for rejection by many; it is rejection which now, as in the past, leads the Christians to preach to the Gentiles. This rejection became a source of mystery to the early Christians: why is it that so many of

the chosen people reject God's Chosen One? One answer,
which only suggests the deepest of mysteries, is given here:
to those predestined by God does the word of God make
sense and by them it finds acceptance; John's Gospel notes
that those believe in Jesus "who are first taught by my
Father."

Influential women and men now persecute Paul and
Barnabas, as was Jesus persecuted in his day by the influential people. In accord with Jesus' advice, the disciples pro-
test unbelief by shaking the dust from their feet; they also
find joy, as Jesus had urged them, in their suffering for him.

14

Paul and Barnabas Preach in Iconium, Lystra, Derbe and Perga, Then Return to Antioch with Their Work Completed

Still performing that work for which the Holy Spirit had called them, Paul and Barnabas, under pressure from citizens of Antioch in Pisidia, turn due eastward to a town called Iconium (about eighty miles from Antioch in Pisidia). At this point Paul is about one hundred and forty miles west of his hometown of Tarsus. From this one can gather that Paul moved somewhat cautiously away from territory he knew very well into territory which was not totally foreign to him.

Luke seesaws between summaries of Paul's efforts in preaching in some towns and particular, notable experiences he had in others. This mix of descriptions, sometimes summary and sometimes anecdotal, was a quality much cherished by those who undertook narrative, historical writing such as we find in the Gospels and in Acts.

In Iconium Paul, as usual, began his work by going to the synagogue; here he tried to be convincing to Jews and Greeks, no doubt by pressing the relationship he saw between Jesus and the Jewish Scriptures. It is Luke's constant effort to show, from Jesus' life, that Jesus is the most plausible fulfillment of the law and prophets. Paul and Barnabas were gifted with powers to work signs and wonders, those miracles which were understood to be expressions of salvation from the powers of this world. At least that is how a Christian would have understood them, and thus Luke called them that, but the prolonged efforts of the disciples won

14 Now at Iconium they entered together into the Jewish synagogue, and so spoke that a great company believed, both of Jews and of Greeks. [2]But the unbelieving Jews stirred up the Gentiles and poisoned their minds against the brethren. [3]So they remained for a long time, speaking boldly for the Lord, who bore witness to the word of his grace, granting signs and wonders to be done by their hands. [4]But the people of the city were divided; some sided with the Jews, and some with the apostles. [5]When an attempt was made by both Gentiles and Jews, with their rulers, to molest them and to stone them, [6]they learned of it and fled to Lystra and Derbe, cities of Lycaonia, and to the surrounding country; [7]and there they preached the gospel.

8 Now at Lystra there was a man sitting, who could not use his feet; he was a cripple from birth, who had never walked. [9]He listened to Paul speaking; and Paul, looking intently at him and seeing that he had faith to be made well, [10]said in a loud voice, "Stand upright on your feet." And he sprang up and walked. [11]And when the crowds saw what Paul had done, they lifted up their voices, saying in Lycaonian, "The gods have come down to us in the likeness of men!" [12]Barnabas they called Zeus, and Paul, because he was the chief speaker, they called Hermes. [13]And the priest of Zeus, whose temple was in front of the city, brought oxen and garlands to the gates and wanted to offer sacrifice with the people. [14]But when the apostles Barnabas and Paul heard of it, they tore their garments and rushed out among the multitude, crying, [15]"Men, why are you doing this? We also are men, of like

nature with you, and bring you good news, that you should turn from these vain things to a living God who made the heaven and the earth and the sea and all that is in them. [16]In past generations he allowed all the nations to walk in their own ways; [17]yet he did not leave himself without witness, for he did good and gave you from heaven rains and fruitful seasons, satisfying your hearts with food and gladness." [18]With these words they scarcely restrained the people from offering sacrifice to them.

19 But Jews came there from Antioch and Iconium; and having persuaded the people, they stoned Paul and dragged him out of the city, supposing that he was dead. [20]But when the disciples gathered about him, he rose up and entered the city; and on the next day he went on with Barnabas to Derbe. [21]When they had preached the gospel to that city and had made many disciples, they returned to Lystra and to Iconium and to Antioch, [22]strengthening the souls of the disciples, exhorting them to continue in the faith, and saying that through many tribulations we must enter the kingdom of God. [23]And when they had appointed elders for them in every church, with prayer and fasting, they committed them to the Lord in whom they believed.

24 Then they passed through Pisidia, and came to Pamphylia. [25]And when they had spoken the word in Perga, they went down to Attalia; [26]and from there they sailed to Antioch, where they had been commended to the grace of God for the work which they had fulfilled. [27]And when they arrived, they gathered the church together and declared all that God had done with them, and how he had opened a door of faith to the Gentiles. [28]And they remained no little time with the disciples.

over at most half the people; we do not know how many of these became Christians. It was a plot to stone and abuse them that caused Paul and Barnabas to flee Iconium. They go south for about twenty-five miles to the smaller town of Lystra.

As Jesus had cured a lame man, lowered to him through a roof, as Peter had cured a man lame from the womb who sat at the Beautiful Gate of the temple, so now Paul mirrors his predecessors by curing a lame man, crippled from birth. It is clear that we are among people who are pagan, not Jewish; their identification of Barnabas with Zeus (supreme god of all Greek gods) and of Paul with Hermes (the god who gave the gift of oratory to human beings) shows their instinctive way of thinking to be pagan. Also, these people wanted to offer sacrifice to them, as though their miracle had revealed them to be gods. (Even today in the fields of Lystra one will find stones on which are carved faces of oxen draped with garlands.)

Though Luke in his storytelling had emphasized that the miracle was in response to the lame man's faith (presumably in the Jesus about whom Paul was at that moment preaching), his speech to ward off the sacrifices of the Lystreans speaks only of God. When one compares this briefer speech to what Paul says to the pagans at the Areopagus in Athens (Acts 17), one sees a repeated way of approach to pagans which may have been used by Jews as well as by Christians. The method is to make the pagans look to the source of their world, to the source of its unity and of the blessings that come to it and from it, that come to all human beings. Paul had begun this way with Cornelius, too. First one is to establish the common bond between speaker and audience—the common bond is God, whose presence, powers and gifts all can easily acknowledge; then one can insert into this divine framework God's will that should appeal to those who recognize God's divine control over creation and his good will toward it.

The speech at Lystra, which barely spared Paul and Barnabas from the adoration due only to God, did produce some good effects, as Paul tried to make clear to the people that God was finally entering their lives as never before, with his offer of salvation through Jesus. Disciples were made here. Yet, the opponents of Iconium hurried to Lystra to upset things, and succeeded to the extent that Paul almost died from a stoning and the mission here had to be abruptly terminated. Paul and Barnabas left quickly for Derbe, a town about thirty miles southeast of Lystra.

The mission at Derbe is very briefly described, though it is noted that many disciples were made there. Paul and Barnabas seem not to have been persecuted in Derbe, but leave on their own accord. As they begin to head back to their community in Antioch in Syria, they sum up for their newly-made disciples the principle they have come to appreciate: one is to undergo many trials, placed in one's path by many enemies, but if one perseveres, one will enter the kingdom of God; given the way of the world, one can expect to enter the kingdom only after experiencing much opposition and trial, for people will test you always.

As Paul and Barnabas retraced their steps—from Derbe, through Lystra and Iconium, to Antioch—they gave their best encouragement to those who had accepted the Lordship of Jesus; they also took the prudent decision to leave older, responsible people from these converts to represent them. In this way, "elders" or "presbyters" (from the Greek word *presbuteroi*) became a regular feature of these communities; these appointments, it should be noted, were not made while Paul was active and preaching in these towns, but were chosen after these people were Christians for some time and as replacements for the disciples as they left the area. In this way, however, we note the ever-lengthening extension of authoritative witnessing: from Jesus to the Twelve, from the Seven, from the Hellenist Jewish Christians and Paul and Barnabas to elders who never knew Jesus, the Old Testament or Yahweh.

Having preached again in the towns they had visited earlier, Paul and Barnabas went to Perga (where they had first landed from Cyprus), preached there, then entered the port of Attalia, just a few miles from Perga; there they found a ship which was going to Antioch in Syria, a sea-journey of about three hundred and twenty miles.

Luke concludes this first missionary enterprise on the Turkish mainland, among the pagans and Jews, by noting Paul's conviction that God had opened the door of faith to the Gentiles. This emphasis does not deny that Jews, too, were converted, but it does call attention to the fact that what even Simeon had predicted about Jesus—a light to the Gentiles—is finally coming true. Luke does not forget to complete the promises he had sown earlier in his works.

We cannot close our comments on this chapter without calling attention to what has, through Luke's way of story-telling, become a fixed pattern. It is the pattern made up of the following elements: visit to a new town, particularly a visit to the local synagogue, preaching and combing of the Jewish Scriptures in relation to the Jesus event, some enthusiastic response, some converts, slow-growing opposition, jealousy or other causes leading to persecution and dismissal, departure from the town, and on to a new opportunity. This was, in many ways, the sequel Jesus came to experience. In reproducing Jesus' experiences the disciples begin to give a kind of witness which is more than verbal; it is the witness of one's fidelity, one's life. One finds that to preach him and accept him is to meet with those forces which opposed him; one can expect, then, persecution for

one's belief. Had not Jesus indicated this as a realistic expectation for those who witnessed to him? Paul's life ex-
emplified the life of his Master in very significant ways; for
this reason Luke follows Paul rather than limit himself to
following the exploits only of founders of communities. Acts
had begun with a summary of the Gospel as "all that Jesus
did and taught." One is tempted to interpret "all that Jesus
did" as a reference to his miracles. However, given Luke's
interest in how the disciple's life mirrors that of Jesus, it is
not wrong to think of the Gospel as a story interested in
the acts of perseverance which Jesus performed and which
would serve to encourage and inspire his followers, Luke's
readers.

15

What Is Necessary for Salvation? Paul and
Barnabas Go to Antioch • Then Paul Begins
His Second Missionary Journey

We have thus far followed two intertwining elements
at the center of Luke's writings. First, there is the geographical element, from Jesus' Galilee to Jerusalem (to the right
hand of the Father), to the disciples' witnessing in Jerusalem,
Judea and Samaria, in Turkey (and to the ends of the earth).
Second, there is the "ethnic" movement, from the Jews of
Galilee and Jerusalem, to the Hellenist Jews and Samaritans,
to religious Gentiles (the Ethiopian eunuch and Cornelius,
the centurion), to the Jews of the diaspora and to pagan
Gentiles. On this latter point, Luke slowly but surely begins
to show the full meaning of the word "everyone" in such a
key statement for his writings as: "Everyone who calls on
the name of the Lord will be saved." With the Cornelius
story God makes absolutely clear that Gentiles, contrary to
the presuppositions of Jewish tradition, are clean in God's
eyes, that God-given faith in Jesus cleanses the pagan's heart.
But there is one more affirmation which must be shouted
out as God's message to the Gentiles (and Jews, as well,
actually), before Luke will be content simply to follow the
geographical movement which serves as the thread for all
his stories to hang upon. It is now that Luke attends to this
affirmation.

To a number of Christians in Jerusalem, the conversion
of Gentiles was a wonderful thing, but these Christians
thought it was the will of God that all converts, Gentile as

SCRIPTURE TEXT

15 But some men came down from Judea and were teaching the brethren, "Unless you are circumcised according to the custom of Moses, you cannot be saved." [2]And when Paul and Barnabas had no small dissension and debate with them, Paul and Barnabas and some of the others were appointed to go up to Jerusalem to the apostles and the elders about this question. [3]So, being sent on their way by the church, they passed through both Phoenicia and Samaria, reporting the conversion of the Gentiles, and they gave great joy to all the brethren. [4]When they came to Jerusalem, they were welcomed by the church and the apostles and the elders, and they declared all that God had done with them. [5]But some believers who belonged to the party of the Pharisees rose up, and said, "It is necessary to circumcise them, and to charge them to keep the law of Moses."

6 The apostles and the elders were gathered together to consider this matter. [7]And after there had been much debate, Peter rose and said to them, "Brethren, you know that in the early days God made choice among you, that by my mouth the Gentiles should hear the word of the gospel and believe. [8]And God who knows the heart bore witness to them, giving them the Holy Spirit just as he did to us; [9]and he made no distinction between us and them, but cleansed their hearts by faith. [10]Now therefore why do you make trial of God by putting a yoke upon the neck of the disciples which neither our fathers nor we have been able to bear? [11]But we believe that we shall be saved through the grace of the Lord Jesus, just as they will."

12 And all the assembly kept silence; and they listened to Barnabas and Paul as they related what signs and wonders God had done through them among the Gentiles. [13]After they finished speaking, James replied, "Brethren, listen to me. [14]Simeon has related how God first visited the Gentiles, to take out of them a people for his name. [15]And with this the words of the prophets agree, as it is written,

> [16]"After this I will return,
>   and I will rebuild the dwelling of David, which
>   has fallen;
>   I will rebuild its ruins,
>   and I will set it up,
> [17]that the rest of men may seek the Lord,
>   and all the Gentiles who are called by my name,
> [18]says the Lord, who has made these things known
>   from of old.'

[19]Therefore my judgment is that we should not trouble those of the Gentiles who turn to God, [20]but should write to them to abstain from the pollutions of idols and from unchastity and from what is strangled and from blood. [21]For from early generations Moses has had in every city those who preach him, for he is read every sabbath in the synagogues."

22 Then it seemed good to the apostles and the elders, with the whole church, to choose men from among them and send them to Antioch with Paul and Barnabas. They sent Judas called Barsabbas, and Silas, leading men among the brethren, [23]with the following letter: "The brethren, both the apostles and the elders, to the brethren who are of the Gentiles in Antioch and Syria and Cilicia, greeting. [24]Since we have heard that some persons from us have troubled you with words, unsettling your minds, although we gave them no in-

structions, [25]it has seemed good to us, having come to one accord, to choose men and send them to you with our beloved Barnabas and Paul, [26]men who have risked their lives for the sake of our Lord Jesus Christ. [27]We have therefore sent Judas and Silas, who themselves will tell you the same things by word of mouth. [28]For it has seemed good to the Holy Spirit and to us to lay upon you no greater burden than these necessary things: [29]that you abstain from what has been sacrificed to idols and from blood and from what is strangled and from unchastity. If you keep yourselves from these, you will do well. Farewell."

30 So when they were sent off, they went down to Antioch; and having gathered the congregation together, they delivered the letter. [31]And when they read it, they rejoiced at the exhortation. [32]And Judas and Silas, who were themselves prophets, exhorted the brethren with many words and strengthened them. [33]And after they had spent some time, they were sent off in peace by the brethren to those who had sent them. [35]But Paul and Barnabas remained in Antioch, teaching and preaching the word of the Lord, with many others also.

36 And after some days Paul said to Barnabas, "Come, let us return and visit the brethren in every city where we proclaimed the word of the Lord, and see how they are." [37]And Barnabas wanted to take with them John called Mark. [38]But Paul thought best not to take with them one who had withdrawn from them in Pamphylia, and had not gone with them to the work. [39]And there arose a sharp contention, so that they separated from each other; Barnabas took Mark with him and sailed away to Cyprus, [40]but Paul chose Silas and departed, being commended by the brethren to the grace of the Lord.

[41]And he went through Syria and Cilicia, strengthening the churches.

well as Jewish, needed to be circumcised and to keep the
Mosaic law to be saved. What this set of obligations implies
is that it is not enough to call on the name of the Lord to
be saved, but that to that call one must add the obligations
of the Jewish religion. The reader need consider only his
own way of life today as a Christian to realize how important
was the resolution of this problem: Is Jesus all that is necessary for salvation, or is he to be supplemented by other
"necessaries"? Note that the question at issue is not whether
or not one may, if one chooses, practice religious characteristics of Judaism such as circumcision, worship in the Jerusalem temple, or the laws of purity; the question is not
what one *may* do, but what one *must* do as a Christian to
be saved.

The demand that Gentile Christians be circumcised and
made to keep the entire Mosaic law was a demand from
those Jews (actually Pharisees) who had become Christians
and were members of the Jerusalem community; presumably
their thinking was that one thousand years of God's revelation of his will for salvation should be integrated with belief in Jesus and the total be presented as what is required
for salvation.

The argument against the "circumcision" position is
twofold; first there are the experiences of Peter and of Paul
and Barnabas, and then there is the interpretation of Scripture by James, the brother of the Lord and immediate leader
of the Jerusalem community. Peter's argument, based on the
fact that he has been the one chosen by God to preach to
the Gentiles ahead of all others, is drawn from his experience with Cornelius: Not only had Cornelius been a friend
of God (contrary to Jewish expectations about Gentiles),
but now Peter draws the conclusion that God never asked
that, once Cornelius was baptized, he should be circumcised
and made to keep the entire Mosaic law. In support of

Peter's argument is that of Paul and Barnabas, drawn from experiences of chapters 13 and 14 of Acts: no Gentile was ever required to be circumcised or made to keep the entire law of Moses—at least those converted appeared to have done all that was necessary for salvation, for enjoyment of God's friendship and a share in his Spirit. If God had not been pleased with these converts, if he had wanted more, he would have made this clear, and he would not have given them the signs of salvation, as he had done.

James' argument shows that what Peter had experienced was already anticipated in the Jewish Scriptures, which represent the mind of God. The key element of this scriptural passage is the clause, "all the Gentiles upon whom my name has been called." This clause is read to mean that "my name" and nothing more is required for entry into God's people, for entry into the "hut" of David which has been destroyed and now is being rebuilt by God himself.

Luke's favorite forms of arguments are based on experience (= what is seen and heard, which are correlatives of what is said and done—things which cannot be denied) and on the Jewish Scriptures. Acts is filled with these forms of argument, and so this chapter's forms of arguments are very common to Luke.

Having decided that the Gentiles need not be circumcised and be held to the entire Mosaic law in order to be saved, James and the rest of the Jerusalem leaders (apostles and presbyters), with the support of the rest of the Church and guided by the Holy Spirit, write to inform the Gentile Christians of Antioch of their decision. They add, however, four elements of the Mosaic law which the Gentile Christians should observe. These four elements are things which were very abhorrent to Jews (even Jewish Christians) of the time; thus, though they might not be necessary for salvation, to perform them would be a sure way of breaking up a Christian community of Jewish and Gentile Christians. A particular word is due here about "illicit sexual union," the element ranked second by James in his speech and fourth in his letter. Are we here talking about something which the Gentile Christians avoid only because the Jewish Christians observe it? Yes. James is referring to the Jewish practice (outlined in Leviticus 17) of avoiding marrying certain very close and physically related persons, e.g., brother, sister, first cousin. The Gentiles were not always as strict about this as were the Jews. Now they are asked to observe this law, rooted in Jewish observance, in order to maintain their Christian community—not because the observance of the entire levitical law is required for salvation.

That this whole affair is decided by the Jerusalem Church underlines the validity of what is done by communities which never knew Jesus or his teaching and thus would not be so capable to draw correct conclusions from it, as has the Jerusalem Church. Though it is said later on in Acts that Paul did teach the contents of the Jerusalem letter to all his converts, there is no record in any of his own letters that he knew of this list of prescriptions. One might note that though Paul did not speak of a list of four prescriptions, he does on occasion teach things which are teachings of the Mosaic law, even to telling the Corinthians to avoid eating meat that is in the process of being offered to idols. But most important to note is that the Jerusalem letter agrees with Pauline teaching: it is only the name of Jesus which saves; the system by which one was to be saved by obedience to the Mosaic law (without Jesus) is to be abandoned. The law does indeed show one way to God, but it cannot give one strength to obey it, it cannot make adequate reparation for infractions, and it needs further adjustment so that it perfectly reflects God's will—for these three correctives, one absolutely needs Jesus, as one looks to him for strength, expiation, the perfect understanding of God's will. Moreover, that Jesus entered the new age means that his followers enter it with him, to the extent they can while remaining in this age; they are, in other words, risen already to a degree, gifted with a life which the Mosaic system could not provide. In this new understanding of salvation, Paul and Acts agree that Jesus is the sole agent of a human being's salvation.

To bring the Jerusalem letter to Antioch Judas and Silas are chosen; with them go Barnabas and Paul. The letter is received with great joy and acceptance; Paul and Barnabas continue their accustomed roles as teachers and preachers in Antioch.

But one day Paul decides to revisit the converts of Turkey; he invites Barnabas, but Barnabas, in a row over John Mark, goes only to Cyprus. It is Silas who becomes the companion of Paul for the visits to the areas near Antioch and Paul's Tarsus.

16

Paul, with Silas and Timothy, Travels the Breadth of Turkey, Then Is Called to Evangelize Macedonia • *Paul in Philippi*

Paul, with Silas, has traveled through the territories surrounding Antioch and Tarsus, the former being in Syria and the latter being in Cilicia. Paul then moved to visit churches of which we heard in Acts 14: churches of Derbe (about one hundred and ten miles west of Tarsus) and of Lystra. It is in Lystra that Paul finds Timothy, who will turn out to be one of Paul's most faithful and famous assistants and will be the recipient of two letters which belong forever to the New Testament: the First and Second Letters to Timothy. Timothy, according to these trustworthy letters, eventually is situated in Ephesus by Paul in order to protect the Ephesian community from false teachings about salvation. Indeed, it is the shoring up of the Christian communities Paul had already founded that motivates Paul's revisiting these young communities. As we have noted before, Luke is perpetually concerned to show that the purity of the salvific message is preserved through links to authorized, accurate witnesses.

Paul asked Timothy to be circumcised, on the basis that Timothy's mother (and not his father) was Jewish. If Timothy, born of a Jewish mother, were not circumcised, he would be shunned by Jews for his apparent disregard for his traditions. Paul, aware of the distinction between circumcision as an ethnic tradition and circumcision as a requirement necessary for salvation, encourages Timothy to be circumcised; this act gives Timothy an entrée to his fellow

SCRIPTURE TEXT

16 And he came also to Derbe and to Lystra. A disciple was there, named Timothy, the son of a Jewish woman who was a believer; but his father was a Greek. ²He was well spoken of by the brethren at Lystra and Iconium. ³Paul wanted Timothy to accompany him; and he took him and circumcised him because of the Jews that were in those places, for they all knew that his father was a Greek. ⁴As they went on their way through the cities, they delivered to them for observance the decisions which had been reached by the apostles and elders who were at Jerusalem. ⁵So the churches were strengthened in the faith, and they increased in numbers daily.

6 And they went through the region of Phrygia and Galatia, having been forbidden by the Holy Spirit to speak the word in Asia. ⁷And when they had come opposite Mysia, they attempted to go into Bithynia, but the Spirit of Jesus did not allow them; ⁸so, passing by Mysia, they went down to Troas. ⁹And a vision appeared to Paul in the night: a man of Macedonia was standing beseeching him and saying, "Come over to Macedonia and help us." ¹⁰And when he had seen the vision, immediately we sought to go on into Macedonia, concluding that God had called us to preach the gospel to them.

11 Setting sail therefore from Troas, we made a direct voyage to Samothrace, and the following day to Neapolis, ¹²and from there to Philippi, which is the leading city of the district of Macedonia, and a Roman colony. We remained in this city some days; ¹³and on the sabbath day we went outside the gate to the riverside, where we supposed there was a place of prayer; and we sat down

and spoke to the women who had come together. ¹⁴One who heard us was a woman named Lydia, from the city of Thyatira, a seller of purple goods, who was a worshiper of God. The Lord opened her heart to give heed to what was said by Paul. ¹⁵And when she was baptized, with her household, she besought us, saying, "If you have judged me to be faithful to the Lord, come to my house and stay." And she prevailed upon us.

16 As we were going to the place of prayer, we were met by a slave girl who had a spirit of divination and brought her owners much gain by soothsaying. ¹⁷She followed Paul and us, crying, "These men are servants of the Most High God, who proclaim to you the way of salvation." ¹⁸And this she did for many days. But Paul was annoyed, and turned and said to the spirit, "I charge you in the name of Jesus Christ to come out of her." And it came out that very hour.

19 But when her owners saw that their hope of gain was gone, they seized Paul and Silas and dragged them into the market place before the rulers; ²⁰and when they had brought them to the magistrates they said, "These men are Jews and they are disturbing our city. ²¹They advocate customs which it is not lawful for us Romans to accept or practice." ²²The crowd joined in attacking them; and the magistrates tore the garments off them and gave orders to beat them with rods. ²³And when they had inflicted many blows upon them, they threw them into prison, charging the jailer to keep them safely. ²⁴Having received this charge, he put them into the inner prison and fastened their feet in the stocks.

25 But about midnight Paul and Silas were praying and singing hymns to God, and the prisoners were listening to them, ²⁶and suddenly there was a great earthquake, so that the foundations of the prison were shaken; and

immediately all the doors were opened and every one's fetters were unfastened. [27]When the jailer woke and saw that the prison doors were open, he drew his sword and was about to kill himself, supposing that the prisoners had escaped. [28]But Paul cried with a loud voice, "Do not harm yourself, for we are all here." [29]And he called for lights and rushed in, and trembling with fear he fell down before Paul and Silas, [30]and brought them out and said, "Men, what must I do to be saved?" [31]And they said, "Believe in the Lord Jesus, and you will be saved, you and your household." [32]And they spoke the word of the Lord to him and to all that were in his house. [33]And he took them the same hour of the night, and washed their wounds, and he was baptized at once, with all his family. [34]Then he brought them up into his house, and set food before them; and he rejoiced with all his household that he had believed in God.

35 But when it was day, the magistrates sent the police, saying, "Let those men go." [36]And the jailer reported the words to Paul, saying, "The magistrates have sent to let you go; now therefore come out and go in peace." [37]But Paul said to them, "They have beaten us publicly, uncondemned, men who are Roman citizens, and have thrown us into prison; and do they now cast us out secretly? No! let them come themselves and take us out." [38]The police reported these words to the magistrates, and they were afraid when they heard that they were Roman citizens; [39]so they came and apologized to them. And they took them out and asked them to leave the city. [40]So they went out of the prison, and visited Lydia; and when they had seen the brethren, they exhorted them and departed.

Jews. Luke notes now that Paul, Silas and Timothy move among the towns of the area, leaving with the Christians the letter from Jerusalem regarding what is the only thing required for salvation (calling on the name of Jesus) and the advice about those things which will promote greater union with Jewish Christians.

Traveling through the heartland of modern Turkey, Paul found that he was prevented from going into the northern parts of the country and understood that this prevention was due to the Spirit of Jesus. (That the Holy Spirit is identified— for the only time in Luke's works, it is true—as the Spirit of Jesus should warn us against tendencies to separate the activities of the Spirit from the continued mission of Jesus the Savior and encourage us to coordinate and interrelate the saving works of these two persons. As a hint of this, one notes how Luke gives the power of Pentecost to the Spirit, but with the understanding that Jesus pours out the Spirit, and thus is responsible in his own way for the effects of the Spirit. Similarly, it is the Spirit who sets apart, in Acts 13, Barnabas and Paul for a specific work, but this occurs only after Luke has made it clear that it is Jesus who is the source and ground of all the witness Paul will do regarding salvation.)

Under the guidance of the Spirit of Jesus, Paul reaches Troas, about eight hundred miles distant from Antioch in Syria where Paul began this journey. This Troas is not to be confused with the Troy of Homer and Vergil, though the two are not far apart. It is at Troas that Paul saw the Macedonian calling for Paul's message to be preached in Macedonia, a country bordering Greece on the north, a country most famous perhaps for the father and son: Philip of Macedon and his son, Alexander the Great (died 323 B.C.). This dream is interpreted as God's will that the message of the Lord be preached in Europe; Paul and his companions set

sail as soon as possible, and Luke brings them quickly past
the island of Samothrace and through the port town of Neapolis (the name "Naples" is derived from this word) to the
major city of Philippi, some one hundred and thirty miles
northwest of Troas.

Paul always liked to go to important city centers, and
Philippi was no exception. It was the major city of its north-
eastern district of Macedonia, named after its famous founder, Philip of Macedon. Conquered by Rome in 167 B.C., it
was in 42 B.C. the site of the famous defeat of Brutus and
Cassius, who killed Julius Caesar. After this famous defeat,
Rome allowed many veterans of its army to settle in Philippi,
thus giving to the city both privileges and strictly Roman
rule. Philippi lies along the main road, the Via Egnatiana,
connecting Rome with Byzantium; Philippi could not help
being famous and rich. Luke chooses to narrate three events
of Paul's stay in Philippi.

There is no mention in the stories of Philippi that Paul
associated with the synagogue, if there was one, in Philippi.
With his companions he searches out a place of prayer on
the sabbath on the bank of a river. It was here that Paul
apparently makes his first converts, some women, of whom
one is mentioned by name: Lydia. This lady is representative
to Philippi on behalf of her fellow citizens in Thyatira, about
two hundred and fifty miles southeast of Philippi, in present-
day Turkey. Thyatira was indeed renowned for its purple
dyes and goods (and it was also known to the Book of Revelation as a city in which the secrets of Satan were studied).
Lydia represented these textile interests and was a person,
like Cornelius, who already knew the true God and thus was
able to respond quickly to the saving message from that
God. It was in her house actually that Paul and his companions stayed, probably to form the beginnings of the first
Christian community in Philippi.

From the baptism of Lydia Luke moves to a rather bizarre story concerning a girl who had a spirit by which she could tell secrets, the future, fortunes. Her talent made it possible to identify the truth about Paul, that he really was a representative of the true God and had a message concerning a way of salvation for the Philippians. The girl hounded Paul and his companions to the point that Paul drives out the demonic spirit which possessed her. Like Jesus before him, Paul does not welcome the witness of demons about his identity; it seems that demonic witness is witness without faith, and for this reason it is unwelcome.

Paul was immediately successful in driving out the spirit, for he used the one name to which the demonic world responded with fear and alacrity: Jesus Christ, Lord of all worlds. The girl, however, is left without the wondrous spirit, and her masters are left without the income they derived from using her to tell fortunes. Even non-believers must adjust to the power of Jesus. The adjustment made in this instance, however, was to have Paul and Silas arrested and eventually flogged and put in jail for a night. The charges were two: disturbing the peace (which usually merited a whipping) and encouragement to Romans to practice customs associated with Judaism, customs which were forbidden to Romans to adopt or engage in. (This latter charge probably refers to the Philippians' perception of the Christian way of salvation and belief in the Jew, Jesus, as "Jewish customs insidious to Roman life.")

The final story, in which Paul and Silas show themselves to be not criminals interested in their own escape, but obedient to Roman law (thus proving the uprightness and peaceful intentions of Christianity), ends in conversion of the jailer who cannot help but marvel at the virtue of these prisoners, at their piety, at the charity they exhibit towards him. Such is the witness operative in this conversion which moved the jailer to the witness to the word of God.

To whip a Roman citizen outside Rome is a crime. It is

not surprising, then, that the authorities of Philippi eagerly freed Paul and Silas with the hope that they would not report them for their mistake. Paul does not intend to report them, but he does demand justice for himself and for the cause for which he labors. This justice is duly given.

It should be noted that Luke's story concerning the crossing from Troas to Macedonia, the story about Lydia and the story about the expulsion of the demon are told in the first person; this feature will be repeated again and more than once. Does it mean that the author of Acts was actually witness to what he describes in the first person? Many, though not all, scholars would say "yes."

17

Trials, Successes, Preaching and Failures of Paul as He Visits Thessalonica, Beroea and Athens

Having left a Christian community at Philippi, sure members of which were Lydia and the jailer and his household, Paul, Silas and Timothy journey westward to the town of Thessalonica, some one hundred miles from Philippi. In Thessalonica we get a glimpse once again of how Paul tried to spread the word of salvation. He is pictured as visiting the synagogue on three successive Saturdays, to discuss with Jews and Gentiles won over to Judaism the meaning and implications of their Scriptures. It is interesting to note how Luke here divides Paul's approach into two parts. First, Paul, without reference to Jesus, shows that the expected Messiah of God, though favored by God, was to suffer and die, and that, though he suffered even to dying, God would make him live again. Since Scripture defines the life of the Messiah in these terms, the Messiah could not avoid them; he *had* to die and rise. Second, Paul declares that Jesus of Nazareth fits the expectations of the Scriptures, even to dying and rising from the dead. Thus, Paul concludes: "Jesus is the Messiah!" Upon reflection one can see how much of the New Testament, and especially how most all of the Lucan work, has labored to integrate the events of Jesus' life into the expectations and prophecies of the Old Testament. Surely, the Christians, among themselves and with non-Christians, spent long hours throughout the Mediterranean basin in pro-

17 Now when they had passed through Amphipolis and Apollonia, they came to Thessalonica, where there was a synagogue of the Jews. ²And Paul went in, as was his custom, and for three weeks he argued with them from the scriptures, ³explaining and proving that it was necessary for the Christ to suffer and to rise from the dead, and saying, "This Jesus, whom I proclaim to you, is the Christ." ⁴And some of them were persuaded, and joined Paul and Silas; as did a great many of the devout Greeks and not a few of the leading women. ⁵But the Jews were jealous, and taking some wicked fellows of the rabble, they gathered a crowd, set the city in an uproar, and attacked the house of Jason, seeking to bring them out to the people. ⁶And when they could not find them, they dragged Jason and some of the brethren before the city authorities, crying, "These men who have turned the world upside down have come here also, ⁷and Jason has received them; and they are all acting against the decrees of Caesar, saying that there is another king, Jesus." ⁸And the people and the city authorities were disturbed when they heard this. ⁹And when they had taken security from Jason and the rest, they let them go.

10 The brethren immediately sent Paul and Silas away by night to Beroea; and when they arrived they went into the Jewish synagogue. ¹¹Now these Jews were more noble than those in Thessalonica, for they received the word with all eagerness, examining the scriptures daily to see if these things were so. ¹²Many of them therefore believed, with not a few Greek women of high standing as well as men. ¹³But when the Jews of Thessalo-

nica learned that the word of God was proclaimed by Paul at Beroea also, they came there too, stirring up and inciting the crowds. [14]Then the brethren immediately sent Paul off on his way to the sea, but Silas and Timothy remained there. [15]Those who conducted Paul brought him as far as Athens; and receiving a command for Silas and Timothy to come to him as soon as possible, they departed.

16 Now while Paul was waiting for them at Athens, his spirit was provoked within him as he saw that the city was full of idols. [17]So he argued in the synagogue with the Jews and the devout persons, and in the market place every day with those who chanced to be there. [18]Some also of the Epicurean and Stoic philosophers met him. And some said, "What would this babbler say?" Others said, "He seems to be a preacher of foreign divinities" —because he preached Jesus and the resurrection. [19]And they took hold of him and brought him to the Areopagus, saying, "May we know what this new teaching is which you present? [20]For you bring some strange things to our ears; we wish to know therefore what these things mean." [21]Now all the Athenians and the foreigners who lived there spent their time in nothing except telling or hearing something new.

22 So Paul, standing in the middle of the Areopagus, said: "Men of Athens, I perceive that in every way you are very religious. [23]For as I passed along, and observed the objects of your worship, I found also an altar with this inscription, 'To an unknown god.' What therefore you worship as unknown, this I proclaim to you. [24]The God who made the world and everything in it, being Lord of heaven and earth, does not live in shrines made by man, [25]nor is he served by human hands, as though he needed anything, since he himself gives to all

men life and breath and everything. [26]And he made from one every nation of men to live on all the face of the earth, having determined allotted periods and the boundaries of their habitation, [27]that they should seek God, in the hope that they might feel after him and find him. Yet he is not far from each one of us, [28]for

'In him we live and move and have our being';
as even some of your poets have said,

'For we are indeed his offspring.'

[29]Being then God's offspring, we ought not to think that the Deity is like gold, or silver, or stone, a representation by the art and imagination of man. [30]The times of ignorance God overlooked, but now he commands all men everywhere to repent, [31]because he has fixed a day on which he will judge the world in righteousness by a man whom he has appointed, and of this he has given assurance to all men by raising him from the dead."

32 Now when they heard of the resurrection of the dead, some mocked; but others said, "We will hear you again about this." [33]So Paul went out from among them. [34]But some men joined him and believed, among them Dionysius the Areopagite and a woman named Damaris and others with them.

cesses similar to that of Paul on Saturdays in Thessalonica's synagogue.

With the announcement that some Jews and many Greek men and prominent women of Thessalonica are converted, we hear further reports, as we have come to expect in Luke's presentation of early Christian witnessing, of opposition and persecution. The motive is resentment, presumably a resentment at Paul's turning Jews from their traditional religion and religious practices to Christianity. The persecution here affects more directly those who were converted, particularly a certain Jason (Jason is not a Jewish name) who gave lodging to the preachers. The description of what happened to Jason, short of death, is very similar to the basic elements of earlier trials (e.g., Stephen, Jesus) in Luke's work; this similarity is intentional, most scholars think. Note even the accusation, fitted to attract the attention of the Greek authorities: they claim Jesus is a king (a clear translation of Messiah for Greeks), in defiance of the emperor.

Such was the incitement at Thessalonica that Paul and Silas and Timothy had to escape in night's darkness. They moved along the Via Egnatiana, the main road linking Rome to Byzantium. It was this road, and its wonderful harbor, that made Thessalonica, surrounded by fertile land, a major city of Macedonia. (Philip of Macedon had named the city after his daughter.) Some twenty-five miles west of Thessalonica lies Beroea.

Beroea, not on the seacoast, but along a plentiful river, and bordered on its north by a vast plain (on its south was Mount Olympus of the gods), had its own synagogue. The Jews there gave a great welcome to Paul and his companions; they are recorded here as having spent many days in study of the Jewish Scriptures, precisely to see if what Paul preached was really so. Here many Jews and prominent

Greek men and women came to believe in Jesus, and things seemed to be at their best in a long time. Nevertheless, persecution again becomes part of the disciples' lot, as Jews in Thessalonica hurry over to Beroea to thwart the preaching of Paul. Luke has us rather well accustomed to the pattern of courageous, insightful witnessing in word and a persecution, usually stirred up by certain Jews, which, in turn, leads to entering new frontiers to preach further the salvation God has determined to give the world through Jesus. In this case, Paul is taken immediately to a ship to get him away from Beroea; he sails for Athens, a journey of about three hundred and eighty miles. Silas and Timothy will join him as soon as possible.

The city of Athens, as Paul found it about 50 A.D., was some five hundred years from its preeminence and glory as the mightiest power in the Mediterranean world; other states, other powers had long replaced Athens, and its primacy in the world of art and science, too, had for long suffered. Yet, it seems that Luke takes the opportunity of Paul's visit to Athens to concentrate on the fact of Athen's long and dominant association with human thought at its deepest level, with philosophy—that search of the mind to find happiness in finding the meaning of all things in relation to man. We do learn of a few converts, and Dionysius and Damaris are named, but Luke's main concern in this episode centers on Paul's approach to "the philosophers."

Epicureans and Stoics, despite their different understandings as to how man is to relate to all things in order to be happy, agree on one thing: the traditional gods of Greece and Rome are of no value, but there are forces in the world which man must recognize as able to dominate him, to which man must adjust since he cannot overcome them. It is to this way of thinking that Paul addresses himself.

Paul's approach to these philosophers is typical of

Greek oratory; he conciliates, recognizes their good quality, renders them benevolent and willing to listen. His starting point is an altar dedicated to "The Unknown God." (Archeology has uncovered an altar in Athens dedicated to "The Unknown God.") Paul sees in this dedication the opportunity to do three things. First, he will deny, as the Old Testament denies, that the Reality, described in the altar dedication as "The Unknown God," is contained in a statue of gold or silver and lives in a house and depends on humans for food and drink through offerings or is even like such a statue. With this the philosophers would agree. Second, the Reality, this "Unknown God," is the one who gives life and breath and all else to mankind, the one in whom all live and move and have their very being; this is Paul's way of joining together Yahweh with this sense of the Greeks that there is another god, the Unknown God, beyond all the gods their ancestors had created. The philosophers would probably agree with this. Third, this Reality, who had already limited men's lives, epochs, territorial boundaries, wanted to be searched for—and found, if possible; that he was only dimly and fleetingly perceived and that his moral, natural law was known, but scorned—he merited only one altar among many, whereas he is actually the only true and living God—was to be repented of in this time of history. This Reality now wants his due recognition, he wants his law acknowledged. These philosophers, who had searched for the laws to happiness and for the powers that govern history and totally dominate all human life and happiness, are in sympathy with Paul's presentation; they have recognized a law or series of laws in the natures of things that one violates only at one's peril—they understand "judgment," "penalty for violation of the laws."

So far, Paul has made sense to the philosophers, as he weds Judaism to the instincts of the Greeks. But then he

enters an area which is completely foreign to the Greeks,
an area which they have reasoned should not exist: it is the
area of the resurrection from the dead. Paul indicates that
this Reality, this Unknown God, will judge the world only
through the mediation of a man raised from the dead. To
the Greek way of thinking, to come back to life is simply to
be put back into the same circumstances in which one had
found so much unhappiness. To propose life after death as
the optimum state for enjoying complete happiness is a con-
tradiction, foolishness. Granted one needs life in order to
be happy, one must look for "life" as something else than
simply being raised to live again in life as one had known
it on earth. At this point, it is understandable that some of
the audience sneered, and others wanted more explanation
"some other time."

The Areopagus, that group of officials who draw their
name (Hill of the god Mars) from a former meeting place,
leaves Paul to listen to more new ideas from still other
preachers.

18

Paul Preaches in Corinth and Stays for At Least a Year and a Half, Then Returns to Antioch Via Ephesus • From Antioch Paul Visits Many Turkish Christian Communities • We Meet Apollos

If Paul did not have much success in Athens, his move to Corinth, just fifty miles to the southwest, proved quite successful. Luke notes that Paul stayed in Corinth for eighteen months, "for quite a while." Part of this willingness to stay so long is due, from the way Luke's story indicates, to a vision of the Lord Jesus to Paul. Jesus, who is at the root of Paul's mission of witnessing, has sent Paul his Spirit and will use other means to further Paul's understanding, courage and joy. Now, from a vision Jesus lets Paul know of the strong support Jesus has, and thus Paul will enjoy, in Corinth.

The Corinthian response is very notable, whether we look to Jews or Gentiles. Paul's manner of approach is still basically the same: to go to the synagogue to engage in discussion, particularly centered on the Jewish Scriptures and Jesus' relation to them. Again, emphasis is placed upon the Messiahship of Jesus of Nazareth.

Apart from the encouragement Paul received from Jesus, Paul also had much support from such people as Aquila and Priscilla (or Prisca) and a leading man of the synagogue, Crispus. Aquila and his wife, Priscilla, came originally from Pontus, which is a large area at the northern end of central Turkey and borders the Black Sea. From there they had

141

SCRIPTURE TEXT

18 After this he left Athens and went to Corinth. ²And he found a Jew named Aquila, a native of Pontus, lately come from Italy with his wife Priscilla, because Claudius had commanded all the Jews to leave Rome. And he went to see them; ³and because he was of the same trade he stayed with them, and they worked, for by trade they were tentmakers. ⁴And he argued in the synagogue every sabbath, and persuaded Jews and Greeks.

5 When Silas and Timothy arrived from Macedonia, Paul was occupied with preaching, testifying to the Jews that the Christ was Jesus. ⁶And when they opposed and reviled him, he shook out his garments and said to them, "Your blood be upon your heads! I am innocent. From now on I will go to the Gentiles." ⁷And he left there and went to the house of a man named Titius Justus, a worshiper of God; his house was next door to the synagogue. ⁸Crispus, the ruler of the synagogue, believed in the Lord, together with all his household; and many of the Corinthians hearing Paul believed and were baptized. ⁹And the Lord said to Paul one night in a vision, "Do not be afraid, but speak and do not be silent; ¹⁰for I am with you, and no man shall attack you to harm you; for I have many people in this city." ¹¹And he stayed a year and six months, teaching the word of God among them.

12 But when Gallio was proconsul of Achaia, the Jews made a united attack upon Paul and brought him before the tribunal, ¹³saying, "This man is persuading men to worship God contrary to the law." ¹⁴But when Paul was about to open his mouth, Gallio said to the Jews, "If it were a matter of wrongdoing or vicious crime, I

should have reason to bear with you, O Jews; [15]but since it is a matter of questions about words and names and your own law, see to it yourselves; I refuse to be a judge of these things." [16]And he drove them from the tribunal. [17]And they all seized Sosthenes, the ruler of the synagogue, and beat him in front of the tribunal. But Gallio paid no attention to this.

18 After this Paul stayed many days longer, and then took leave of the brethren and sailed for Syria, and with him Priscilla and Aquila. At Cenchreae he cut his hair, for he had a vow. [19]And they came to Ephesus, and he left them there; but he himself went into the synagogue and argued with the Jews. [20]When they asked him to stay for a longer period, he declined; [21]but on taking leave of them he said, "I will return to you if God wills," and he set sail from Ephesus.

22 When he had landed at Caesarea, he went up and greeted the church, and then went down to Antioch. [23]After spending some time there he departed and went from place to place through the region of Galatia and Phrygia, strengthening all the disciples.

24 Now a Jew named Apollos, a native of Alexandria, came to Ephesus. He was an eloquent man, well versed in the scriptures. [25]He had been instructed in the way of the Lord; and being fervent in spirit, he spoke and taught accurately the things concerning Jesus, though he knew only the baptism of John. [26]He began to speak boldly in the synagogue; but when Priscilla and Aquila heard him, they took him and expounded to him the way of God more accurately. [27]And when he wished to cross to Achaia, the brethren encouraged him, and wrote to the disciples to receive him. When he arrived, he greatly helped those who through grace had believed, [28]for he

powerfully confuted the Jews in public, showing by the scriptures that the Christ was Jesus.

moved to Rome, where there was a sizable community of Jews; it seems that Emperor Claudius (reigned 41–54 A.D.) is recorded as having such trouble with the Jews that he drove them all out of Rome. We do not know exactly when Claudius did this, but according to Luke it was in time for Aquila and Priscilla to cross paths with Paul in 52 A.D. Within five years or so Paul will write his famous Letter to the Romans; surely by the time he reached Corinth there was already a flourishing Christian community in Rome, founded by someone other than Paul. Perhaps the recorded friction between Jewish Christians and Jewish non-Christians in Rome led Claudius to throw up his hands and disperse the Jews, at least for a while. (Jews trace their origins in Rome to a time earlier than 200 B.C.) Perhaps, too, Aquila and Priscilla, who had to leave Rome, were part of the Jewish Christian community and thus were baptized before they reached Corinth; some scholars think, however, that they were some of Paul's earliest converts in Corinth itself. In any event, Paul found them very hospitable and shared their work of tent-making.

Paul also is recorded here as living in the house of a Gentile, Titus Justus; perhaps this man even became a Christian. Soon room had to be made for Silas and Timothy as they finally arrived from Beroea where Paul last saw them.

In Corinth Paul met not only with success, but also with opposition; it is opposition from some of the Jews, who from the discussions with Paul were convinced that he was distorting their traditions and religious faith. This provides Luke with a second occasion (cf. Acts 13:45–47) in which to show in concrete circumstances how the Gentile mission grew in part out of Jewish resistance to and violence toward the preaching. Paul will take up this theme in his own Letter to the Romans, where he notes that the natural shoots of the tree were allowed to grow dry with the result that "foreign" shoots were grafted into the tree. Parables of Jesus had already noted that the man who gave the banquet insisted that his banquet hall be filled with guests, even when the invited ones had refused to come.

A specific instance of Jewish persecution was the arraignment of Paul before the Roman authority of Corinth, the proconsul Gallio. Thanks to an extant ancient inscription we are able to fix this event as occurring sometime in 52 A.D. In fact, this dating is the basis on which we decide that all else that happens to Paul before this Corinthian date is to be dated to a time prior to 52 A.D. What Luke finds important about this trial are the words of Gallio himself. As in so many other trials of Christians (even of Jesus himself), the first reaction of the Roman ruler is to recognize that Christianity is no threat to Rome, but is simply representing a difference of opinion about matters purely internal to Judaism. Many scholars see in such a statement as Gallio's a subtle effort by Luke to provide for any eventual reader of Acts the "official" reaction of earlier Roman authority, a reaction which Luke would like contemporary and future Roman authority to imitate toward Christianity. Because the case against Paul fails, a leading man of the synagogue gets pummeled by the crowd—evidently for failing to argue well enough against Paul. Surely Gallio does not see it as a beginning of a riot, to stem which (the Jews might have plotted) Gallio would have to give in and punish Paul. Such a fear, of course, did move Pontius Pilate to kill Jesus.

Paul's stay in Corinth comes to an end; he with Aquila and Priscilla leave the town to go to its eastern port, from which they leave for Ephesus, some three hundred and fifty miles eastward by boat. The mention of the port Cenchreae suggests that we give a moment's consideration to the city of Corinth whose needs were actually served by two ports.

Greece is divided into two land masses, one north and

one south; what connects them is a narrow neck of land
called the Isthmus of Corinth. It is clear that all land traffic
going north and south into the two parts of Greece and
beyond must pass over this narrow neck; the people who
controlled that neck of land controlled the traffic of all that
passed, north and south, through Greece. Moreover, on either side of the thin neck of land were gulf waters; to the
west was the Gulf of Corinth and to the east was the Saronic
Gulf. Each gulf opened onto the major waters of the Mediterranean, to the west touching Italy and to the east touching Turkey. Most traders between east and west, between
Rome, Spain, France and Turkey, Syria, even to India, preferred to sail into one of the gulfs and have their goods
transferred across the narrow Isthmus of Corinth and re-
loaded onto a ship which would leave from the other gulf.
Again, whoever controlled the neck of land controlled east-
west traffic over the known world. Who controlled this neck
of land? Corinth, of course.

Corinth itself was situated at the south end of the Isthmus, and at a safe distance from either of the gulfs. This
distance meant that Corinth needed locations right at the
waters for the handling of necessities at those points. Thus,
there was a port on the Saronic Gulf which looks toward
Turkey—this was the port of Cenchreae; and there was a
port on the Gulf of Corinth looking toward Rome—this was
the port of Lechaeon. It probably comes as no surprise that
Corinth, destroyed in 146 B.C., was built again by Julius Caesar in 44 B.C. to resume its role as master of the east-west,
north-south trading channels. No surprise either is the fact
that, by Paul's time, Corinth was a place where the whole
world sought to find work; out of these kinds of people of
varying religious and philosophical backgrounds Paul was to
create a community dedicated to Jesus.

Luke refers to Paul's shaving his head at the end of a

period of special dedication to God; the tradition behind this action (cf. Num 6:13.18) is that one does not cut one's hair during the entire period of one's dedication, but only after it.

Luke brings Paul to Ephesus, about three hundred and twenty miles from Corinth, where Paul is only briefly described as entering into those kinds of discussions in the synagogue which we are accustomed to expect. From Ephesus Paul returns to Israel (about six hundred and eight miles by ship), then goes to Antioch in Syria, his "home community," and then begins again, for a third time (about 53/54 A.D.), a prolonged visit through central Turkey to encourage his Christians.

Strength, too, was given, Luke assures us, to the Corinthian community through Apollos, a Jew from Egypt who had the qualities which appeal to Luke: such mastery of Scripture and such accurate knowledge of Christianity that he showed Jesus to be the Messiah.

19

Paul's Experiences in Ephesus

Luke reminds us that Apollos worked in Ephesus before Paul arrived there. Apollos is interesting to us, not only because he will be mentioned prominently in the early chapters of Paul's First Letter to the Corinthians, but because we learn that he, even before becoming a Christian, was well instructed in the new way of life dedicated to Jesus. Who taught Apollos? How did he learn so much and so well? And, even more to the point, how many others were there who reflect the vibrant, energetic, insightful representation of God's new way in Jesus? In inviting us to consider imaginatively what else was happening in these early decades, Luke convinces us more and more that he is being consciously selective in what he gives us, from the earliest chapters of his Gospel to the latest chapters of his Acts of the Apostles. With what he has presented about Jesus and then about the witnessing concerning him, Luke feels that he has been most able to support with vigor those teachings which Theophilus had already received. All material is sifted through and selected by Luke with this goal in mind. If his Gospel and Acts are limited in their material, Luke is not to be faulted; if they do not achieve their stated goal, then Luke has failed.

Paul's arrival in Ephesus brings him into contact with about twelve men who are in the odd situation of being followers of the moral life lived by Christians and of being dedicated to Jesus without ever having been baptized in the name of Jesus and without ever having received the Pen-

SCRIPTURE TEXT

19 While Apollos was at Corinth, Paul passed through the upper country and came to Ephesus. There he found some disciples. ²And he said to them, "Did you receive the Holy Spirit when you believed?" And they said, "No, we have never even heard that there is a Holy Spirit." ³And he said, "Into what then were you baptized?" They said, "Into John's baptism." ⁴And Paul said, "John baptized with the baptism of repentance, telling the people to believe in the one who was to come after him, that is, Jesus." ⁵On hearing this, they were baptized in the name of the Lord Jesus. ⁶And when Paul had laid his hands upon them, the Holy Spirit came on them; and they spoke with tongues and prophesied. ⁷There were about twelve of them in all.

8 And he entered the synagogue and for three months spoke boldly, arguing and pleading about the kingdom of God; ⁹but when some were stubborn and disbelieved, speaking evil of the Way before the congregation, he withdrew from them, taking the disciples with him, and argued daily in the hall of Tyrannus. ¹⁰This continued for two years, so that all the residents of Asia heard the word of the Lord, both Jews and Greeks.

11 And God did extraordinary miracles by the hands of Paul, ¹²so that handkerchiefs or aprons were carried away from his body to the sick, and diseases left them and the evil spirits came out of them. ¹³Then some of the itinerant Jewish exorcists undertook to pronounce the name of the Lord Jesus over those who had evil spirits, saying, "I adjure you by the Jesus whom Paul preaches." ¹⁴Seven sons of a Jewish high priest named

Sceva were doing this. [15]But the evil spirit answered them, "Jesus I know, and Paul I know; but who are you?" [16]And the man in whom the evil spirit was leaped on them, mastered all of them, and overpowered them, so that they fled out of that house naked and wounded. [17]And this became known to all residents of Ephesus, both Jews and Greeks; and fear fell upon them all; and the name of the Lord Jesus was extolled. [18]Many also of those who were now believers came, confessing and divulging their practices. [19]And a number of those who practiced magic arts brought their books together and burned them in the sight of all; and they counted the value of them and found it came to fifty thousand pieces of silver. [20]So the word of the Lord grew and prevailed mightily.

21 Now after these events Paul resolved in the Spirit to pass through Macedonia and Achaia and go to Jerusalem, saying, "After I have been there, I must also see Rome." [22]And having sent into Macedonia two of his helpers, Timothy and Erastus, he himself stayed in Asia for a while.

23 About that time there arose no little stir concerning the Way. [24]For a man named Demetrius, a silversmith, who made silver shrines of Artemis, brought no little business to the craftsmen. [25]These he gathered together, with the workmen of like occupation, and said, "Men, you know that from this business we have our wealth. [26]And you see and hear that not only at Ephesus but almost throughout all Asia this Paul has persuaded and turned away a considerable company of people, saying that gods made with hands are not gods. [27]And there is danger not only that this trade of ours may come into disrepute but also that the temple of the great god-

dess Artemis may count for nothing, and that she may
even be deposed from her magnificence, she whom all
Asia and the world worship."

28 When they heard this they were enraged, and
cried out, "Great is Artemis of the Ephesians!" [29]So the
city was filled with the confusion; and they rushed together into the theater, dragging with them Gaius and
Aristarchus, Macedonians who were Paul's companions
in travel. [30]Paul wished to go in among the crowd, but
the disciples would not let him; [31]some of the Asiarchs
also, who were friends of his, sent to him and begged him
not to venture into the theater. [32]Now some cried one
thing, some another; for the assembly was in confusion,
and most of them did not know why they had come
together. [33]Some of the crowd prompted Alexander,
whom the Jews had put forward. And Alexander motioned with his hand, wishing to make a defense to the
people. [34]But when they recognized that he was a Jew,
for about two hours they all with one voice cried out,
"Great is Artemis of the Ephesians!" [35]And when the town
clerk had quieted the crowd, he said, "Men of Ephesus,
what man is there who does not know that the city of the
Ephesians is temple keeper of the great Artemis, and of
the sacred stone that fell from the sky? [36]Seeing then that
these things cannot be contradicted, you ought to be
quiet and do nothing rash. [37]For you have brought these
men here who are neither sacrilegious nor blasphemers
of our goddess. [38]If therefore Demetrius and the craftsmen with him have a complaint against any one, the
courts are open, and there are proconsuls; let them bring
charges against one another. [39]But if you seek anything
further, it shall be settled in the regular assembly. [40]For
we are in danger of being charged with rioting today,
there being no cause that we can give to justify this

commotion." [41]And when he had said this, he dismissed the assembly.

tecostal effects of the Holy Spirit. Luke is not at pains to
explain more exactly just what this discipleship entailed or
what baptism adds to their chosen way of life; certainly, the
effect of baptism, the outpouring of the Spirit's gifts, is received only after proper baptism. Amidst questions we
would like to ask Luke we should pay attention to the major
point, that the repentance God asks of human beings (John
has made this a central facet of his mediation of God to
mankind) will not, of its own dynamism, give a human being
all that God wants to give him. It is only through the commitment professed in baptism that one receives the fullness
of God: his Holy Spirit. To present baptism as he does here
suggests to some that Luke thinks of baptism as a rite which
is purely external with no meaning in itself. On the contrary,
Luke assumes that the reader knows the difference between
life with and life without baptism; he here wants to underline that repentance alone, following John alone, is to fail to
grasp the plan of God, to know the one through whom salvation is to be had, to enjoy the Spirit of God. In short,
repentance without Jesus will not bring a person the fullness
of God's love and gifts.

Luke notes that Paul discussed for a long time the person of Jesus and his relationship to the Jewish Scriptures;
again woven into this frank series of discussions is the theme
of persecution, this time attributed to obstinacy. The persecution in turn moves Paul ever closer to Gentiles who will
listen to him. Paul's lengthy stay in Ephesus and his willingness to discuss day after day with Jew and Greek alike meant
that the entire west-central portion of Turkey was able to
hear the message. (This large area of Turkey was known in
Paul's times as "Asia Minor," smaller Asia, to be distinguished
from the larger "Asia" of the Far East.) As with Jesus and
Peter at earlier moments, God supports the call to believe

in Jesus with astounding miracles, including the expulsion of demons, the most vile of man's masters.

Control of demons was, for this period of history, probably the most overwhelming power enjoyed by human beings; the degree of Jesus' power over demons is one of the surest suggestions that he is more than human and that with him is present the kingdom of God, who alone can totally subdue Satan. When non-Christians see that the name of Jesus drives out evil spirits, they presume to speak his name to disperse demons. The reaction of the evil spirits underlines the fact that faith in Jesus must be linked with calling on his name in order to save. At the very least, one who uses Jesus' name must have the good intention of bringing about the kingdom of God; with this minimum one will be protected against the counter-attacks of the demons. But to exorcise without the minimum requirement by which one truly represents Jesus, to exorcise without thereafter bringing one to Jesus—this God will not support. Others, too, besides the Jewish exorcists with which the story began, rid themselves of objects and books in which they had put their hope to overcome demons. The name of Jesus and commitment to Jesus is the only means to salvation from evil forces. The immense value of the objects burned underlines the conviction that people did put their hope in Jesus, people from all over Ephesus.

Luke has one more major story to tell, drawn from Paul's three years of work in Ephesus. But he willingly interrupts his concentration on Ephesus to look beyond this city to Macedonia, to Greece—and then to Rome. One sees in this brief look forward that author's way of keeping the reader alert to the dynamism which moves the story of witness inexorably to its pre-ordained goal. Not to be overlooked is Paul's expression that "it is necessary" that he visit

Rome, too. A laconic reference perhaps, but the necessity underlines the divine plan which the reader has come to know in the life of Jesus and in subsequent events. What, of course, is not expressed is "how" Paul will move from Israel to Rome; in this our author is bittersweet: the great goal will be reached, but with what suffering!

The final story about Paul in Ephesus has to do with silver and with Artemis. Artemis, the sister of Apollo and virgin goddess of the hunt, was, in Ephesus, the goddess of fertility. To this goddess was erected one of the seven wonders of the ancient world, the temple of Artemis, a temple fifty yards wide by eighty yards long, placed on a platform eighty yards wide by one hundred and twenty yards long. The columns of the temple, each eighteen yards high, numbered one hundred. Associated with this temple was a theater which held twenty-four thousand people, the largest of its kind in antiquity yet uncovered. Ephesus was a very wealthy city, as it was the chief port and market hub of Turkey when approached from the west. As the center of worship to Artemis, it is no wonder that objects of value were made in her honor and sold to as many as could afford them. The trade in these crafted objects, miniature shrines of the goddess in silver, was brisk and very profitable. Any suggestion that the trade might go out of business was indeed a threat to many people. It is just such a threat that a certain silversmith claimed Paul to be.

Once again, the Christian message is given the role of potential threat to pagan gods, to pagan institutions, as it was construed many times as a threat to Judaism. Here, like Gamaliel in the case of Peter and the other disciples in Jerusalem, a non-Christian speaks words that temper the wilder emotions. The argument about punishment for illegal acts against people who should be judged properly, in a court, is a good one which Luke would like all people to consider before attacking Christianity in mob form. That Luke would agree with the other argument, that Artemis will defend herself and her temple against the true God, with this Luke would not agree. But it is a pagan who says it and it convinces the rioters to withdraw, realizing that Christians of Ephesus were not intent on destroying the temple and were too small in number to hurt the silver trade. It is the effect that Luke desires, the freeing of Christian witness to continue its pre-determined way "to the ends of the earth." It is within such a vast variety of human circumstances, beginning with Jesus himself, that God offers salvation to the whole world. Within these circumstances one sees again that witness is not only verbal; at times it demands even one's life.

20

Paul Moves From Ephesus to Greece Via Macedonia, Then Takes the Same Route Back Through Ephesus to Miletus • Events in Troas and Miletus

After his three-year stay in Ephesus Paul again takes to the road, driven by his preoccupation to encourage all those who had embraced Jesus as their saving Lord. We have seen many times the concern Luke has that we understand the efforts of God and man to encourage and inspire, to console and support those who have begun to walk the way of Christianity. Luke finds this effort to be one of the great hallmarks of charity, of the Church, and an integral part of "witness to Jesus."

Paul passed through Macedonia and came to Greece, where he stayed for three months. He wanted to set sail from Greece (probably from Corinth) to return to Israel, but a plot against his life made him give up the idea of sailing; he took the land route back through Greece and Macedonia to Troas (where Paul had had his vision of the Macedonian, inviting Paul to bring his message of salvation to Macedonia and Greece).

As Paul makes his way from Greece, Luke gives us names of his traveling companions. The list is interesting, for it shows how Paul took with him representatives of many places he had evangelized; since these names do not include all the people who had traveled with Paul on his mission (e.g., Erastus), we can imagine even a larger number who helped Paul, at least at certain moments of his career. Pre-

20After the uproar ceased, Paul sent for the disciples and having exhorted them took leave of them and departed for Macedonia. ²When he had gone through these parts and had given them much encouragement, he came to Greece. ³There he spent three months, and when a plot was made against him by the Jews as he was about to set sail for Syria, he determined to return through Macedonia. ⁴Sopater of Beroea, the son of Pyrrhus, accompanied him; and of the Thessalonians, Aristarchus and Secundus; and Gaius of Derbe, and Timothy; and the Asians, Tychicus and Trophimus. ⁵These went on and were waiting for us at Troas, ⁶but we sailed away from Philippi after the days of Unleavened Bread, and in five days we came to them at Troas, where we stayed for seven days.

7 On the first day of the week, when we were gathered together to break bread, Paul talked with them, intending to depart on the morrow; and he prolonged his speech until midnight. ⁸There were many lights in the upper chamber where we were gathered. ⁹And a young man named Eutychus was sitting in the window. He sank into a deep sleep as Paul talked still longer; and being overcome by sleep, he fell down from the third story and was taken up dead. ¹⁰But Paul went down and bent over him, and embracing him said, "Do not be alarmed, for his life is in him." ¹¹And when Paul had gone up and had broken bread and eaten, he conversed with them a long while, until daybreak, and so departed. ¹²And they took the lad away alive, and were not a little comforted.

13 But going ahead to the ship, we set sail for Assos,

intending to take Paul aboard there; for so he had arranged, intending himself to go by land. [14]And when he met us at Assos, we took him on board and came to Mitylene. [15]And sailing from there we came the following day opposite Chios; the next day we touched at Samos; and the day after that we came to Miletus. [16]For Paul had decided to sail past Ephesus, so that he might not have to spend time in Asia; for he was hastening to be at Jerusalem, if possible, on the day of Pentecost.

17 And from Miletus he sent to Ephesus and called to him the elders of the church. [18]And when they came to him, he said to them:

"You yourselves know how I lived among you all the time from the first day that I set foot in Asia, [19]serving the Lord with all humility and with tears and with trials which befell me through the plots of the Jews; [20]how I did not shrink from declaring to you anything that was profitable, and teaching you in public and from house to house, [21]testifying both to Jews and to Greeks of repentance to God and of faith in our Lord Jesus Christ. [22]And now, behold, I am going to Jerusalem, bound in the Spirit, not knowing what shall befall me there; [23]except that the Holy Spirit testifies to me in every city that imprisonment and afflictions await me. [24]But I do not account my life of any value nor as precious to myself, if only I may accomplish my course and the ministry which I received from the Lord Jesus, to testify to the gospel of the grace of God. [25]And now, behold, I know that all you among whom I have gone preaching the kingdom will see my face no more. [26]Therefore I testify to you this day that I am innocent of the blood of all of you, [27]for I did not shrink from declaring to you the whole counsel of God. [28]Take heed to yourselves and to all the flock, in which the Holy Spirit has made you overseers, to care for the church of God which he obtained with the blood of his own Son. [29]I know that after my departure fierce wolves will come in among you, not sparing the flock; [30]and from among your own selves will arise men speaking perverse things, to draw away the disciples after them. [31]Therefore be alert, remembering that for three years I did not cease night or day to admonish every one with tears. [32]And now I commend you to God and to the word of his grace, which is able to build you up and to give you the inheritance among all those who are sanctified. [33]I coveted no one's silver or gold or apparel. [34]You yourselves know that these hands ministered to my necessities, and to those who were with me. [35]In all things I have shown you that by so toiling one must help the weak, remembering the words of the Lord Jesus, how he said, 'It is more blessed to give than to receive.' "

36 And when he had spoken thus, he knelt down and prayed with them all. [37]And they all wept and embraced Paul and kissed him, [38]sorrowing most of all because of the word he had spoken, that they should see his face no more. And they brought him to the ship.

sumably, these are some of the people who learned the
meaning of Christianity well and thus can be considered as
authoritative and contemporary witnesses to Jesus.

The companions named here go in advance of Paul at
least as far as Troas; their goal, of course, is still Israel, at
least for some of them. With Paul and at a slower pace are
the undefined person(s) signaled in the text by the pronoun
"we." This "we" surfaced earlier, in chapter 16, but then
faded out as abruptly as it was introduced. As mentioned
before, many scholars think that when Luke narrates a section dominated by this "we," he is recalling his own personal
experiences with Paul; other scholars, however, think that
the "we-passages" can be explained in other ways so that
Luke is not included in the "we" expression.

It is interesting to note that Paul joins his traveling companions in Troas after the feast of Unleavened Bread was
completed for that year. Surely such a dating for his departure from Philippi for Troas indicates that Paul waited re-
spectfully until this major Jewish feast was completed before
sailing and that he did this because he wanted to celebrate
the feast (which occurs at the time of Passover) out of respect for his Jewish roots. Paul was able to integrate his
Jewish past into his new understanding of God and Jesus
without denying that Jesus is the one thing necessary for
salvation.

The story of Paul's lengthy sermon in Troas is set within
the framework of a meal on the first day of the week. One
is led to think that Luke intends through these details to
have the Christian think of a eucharistic meal as the back-
drop to Paul's talk with his friends. One element which
makes the story worthy of recital in such a work as Acts,
however, is the continual miracle-working ability of Paul; it
is a miracle-working power which serves not only to spread

the Gospel, but to express sympathy and protection as well. Note how the story ends with the observation that the people were greatly comforted by God's power on behalf of their Eutychus; miracles serve to express love and comfort, as well as to sustain preaching belief in Jesus.

Still in the style of first person ("we") narrative, Luke identifies the various stops of Paul's group made from Troas southward. They reach Assos (by land from Troas about fifteen miles, by sea about forty miles), Mitylene (thirty miles from Assos), Chios (about fifty miles sailing from Mitylene), Samos (about seventy-five miles from Chios), and finally Miletus (about twenty-four miles from Samos). At Miletus, an ancient commercial center at the mouth of the Meander River, Paul stops his journey in order to give an important address to those elders or presbyters of the Church of Ephesus Paul had earlier appointed to guide the Christians there, once he had been convinced that these were indeed the men who could hand on the true witness in his place. These men come from Ephesus, about thirty miles north of Miletus. Paul asks them to come to him, because he did not want to halt in Ephesus lest he be delayed to such a degree that he would miss celebrating Pentecost (the Jewish major feast, seven weeks after Passover) in Jerusalem. Paul had already spent about two weeks traveling since Passover, and still has much sailing to do to make his deadline. Again, we note Paul's interest in celebrating Jewish feasts, even though he is now a Christian.

The address Paul gives to the men he has called to Miletus is intended to inspire and encourage these elders (indeed, anyone with responsibilities like theirs); within the address a number of valuable observations are made.

Paul first insists that he had remained faithful to his role as witness: he, like all before him, had demanded the integration of two essential elements of the will of God—repentance for one's past and faith in Jesus. To this must these men continue to be witnesses.

Paul then reveals his awareness of his own future, a future of chains and hardships. He reveals this, because he, like a dying man, claims he is to be trusted in his assertion that he cannot be blamed for not preaching the word of God in its entirety, in its fullness; he has been an authentic witness. Moreover, he prefers his life of witness to a life without persecution, if life without persecution means that he must limit or deny totally the witness he knows to be authentic.

Paul then turns his attention to the future of these presbyters before him, presbyters, he insists, who have been designated by the Holy Spirit. They are to guard the flock the Spirit has given them to guard, a Church purchased by God with his own blood (who can say that Luke is ignorant of the death of Jesus as a death which rids mankind of its sins, is ignorant of the blood which redeems as God's blood?). Paul warns these men that threats to the flock will come even from within the Church and stresses the threat which has to do with distortion of the truth handed on to the flock. Paul had always warned them of these threats and dangers; he had always been preparing them for these days with great, even tearful insistence. With an eye to these strenuous days ahead Paul commends these elders to the Lord who, if trusted, will by his word build his Church and provide an inheritance for his holy ones. As further encouragement to these men, Paul offers his own example of labor for men's hearts, not for their silver or gold. Indeed, within this series of motivations we learn of a new word of Jesus regarding the happiness of giving: it is a happiness which is greater than that of receiving.

The speech is meant to encourage, but it certainly

caused distress and tears as it announced Paul's definitive departure from his friends. In the light of this growing awareness and sorrow regarding Paul's imminent future which Luke has sown into his narrative and which will become ever more apparent, we can look back on elements of this chapter to see in them Luke's attempt to liken Paul to Jesus—granted the essential differences in the lot of each of them.

Paul has already announced his intention of visiting Rome (Acts 19:21) and sends companions ahead of him to prepare his way. We are given the list of his traveling companions and a story of a sermon the length of which is determined by the fact that he will never see Troas again. Paul reveals his awareness, given him in city after city by the Holy Spirit, of impending, imminent calamity; he prepares for this by leaving behind those chosen through the Holy Spirit. We will note other points of contact between Jesus' last days and those of Paul. The likeness of the one to the other is important for Luke, for that very likeness is a true, profound form of witness.

21

At Two Stations of His Journey, Tyre and Caesarea, Paul Hears Forebodings About His Fate in Jerusalem; in Jerusalem Paul Is Captured in the Temple Area and the Crowd Asks His Death

Paul departs with his friends from Miletus, after a distressing farewell; clearly the emphasis shifts more and more to the imminent capture and imprisonment of Paul, as the source we have become accustomed to in this chapter, the "we-source," relates these events. Luke quickly moves Paul from Miletus past the island of Cos (about fifty miles south of Miletus), then past Rhodes (about one hundred miles south of Cos), to Patara (about ninety miles due east of Rhodes); from Patara, with a change of ship, Paul sails directly to Tyre, some four hundred and eighty miles southeast of Patara.

Paul waited in Tyre for the unloading of the ship. Luke's sole notice about this stay of a week is renewed warning and anxiety about what is clearly being foreseen now by many of the Christians. Paul, like Christ, is to go up to Jerusalem, where, these Tyrian Christians know from the Holy Spirit, Paul will meet the fate Jerusalem held for so many former prophets of God.

From Tyre Paul sailed another forty miles or so to Ptolemais, a port city of northern Palestine which Herod the Great used only as a military port after he had built the greater port of Caesarea-by-the-Sea. From here Paul goes south about forty miles to Caesarea-by-the-Sea, where for the

21 And when we had parted from them and set sail, we came by a straight course to Cos, and the next day to Rhodes, and from there to Patara. [2]And having found a ship crossing to Phoenicia, we went aboard, and set sail. [3]When we had come in sight of Cyprus, leaving it on the left we sailed to Syria, and landed at Tyre; for there the ship was to unload its cargo. [4]And having sought out the disciples, we stayed there for seven days. Through the Spirit they told Paul not to go on to Jerusalem. [5]And when our days there were ended, we departed and went on our journey; and they all, with wives and children, brought us on our way till we were outside the city; and kneeling down on the beach we prayed and bade one another farewell. [6]Then we went on board the ship, and they returned home.

7 When we had finished the voyage from Tyre, we arrived at Ptolemais; and we greeted the brethren and stayed with them for one day. [8]On the morrow we departed and came to Caesarea; and we entered the house of Philip the evangelist, who was one of the seven, and stayed with him. [9]And he had four unmarried daughters, who prophesied. [10]While we were staying for some days, a prophet named Agabus came down from Judea. [11]And coming to us he took Paul's girdle and bound his own feet and hands, and said, "Thus says the Holy Spirit, 'So shall the Jews at Jerusalem bind the man who owns this girdle and deliver him into the hands of the Gentiles.'" [12]When we heard this, we and the people there begged him not to go up to Jerusalem. [13]Then Paul answered, "What are you doing, weeping and breaking my heart?

For I am ready not only to be imprisoned but even to die at Jerusalem for the name of the Lord Jesus." [14]And when he would not be persuaded, we ceased and said, "The will of the Lord be done."

15 After these days we made ready and went up to Jerusalem. [16]And some of the disciples from Caesarea went with us, bringing us to the house of Mnason of Cyprus, an early disciple, with whom we should lodge.

17 When we had come to Jerusalem, the brethren received us gladly. [18]On the following day Paul went in with us to James; and all the elders were present. [19]After greeting them, he related one by one the things that God had done among the Gentiles through his ministry. [20]And when they heard it, they glorified God. And they said to him, "You see, brother, how many thousands there are among the Jews of those who have believed; they are all zealous for the law, [21]and they have been told about you that you teach all the Jews who are among the Gentiles to forsake Moses, telling them not to circumcise their children or observe the customs. [22]What then is to be done? They will certainly hear that you have come. [23]Do therefore what we tell you. We have four men who are under a vow; [24]take these men and purify yourself along with them and pay their expenses, so that they may shave their heads. Thus all will know that there is nothing in what they have been told about you but that you yourself live in observance of the law. [25]But as for the Gentiles who have believed, we have sent a letter with our judgment that they should abstain from what has been sacrificed to idols and from blood and from what is strangled and from unchastity." [26]Then Paul took the men, and the next day he purified himself with them and went into the temple, to give notice when the days of purification

would be fulfilled and the offering presented for every one of them.

27 When the seven days were almost completed, the Jews from Asia, who had seen him in the temple, stirred up all the crowd, and laid hands on him, [28]crying out, "Men of Israel, help! This is the man who is teaching men everywhere against the people and the law and this place; moreover he also brought Greeks into the temple, and he has defiled this holy place." [29]For they had previously seen Trophimus the Ephesian with him in the city, and they supposed that Paul had brought him into the temple. [30]Then all the city was aroused, and the people ran together, they seized Paul and dragged him out of the temple, and at once the gates were shut. [31]And as they were trying to kill him, word came to the tribune of the cohort that all Jerusalem was in confusion. [32]He at once took soldiers and centurions, and ran down to them; and when they saw the tribune and the soldiers, they stopped beating Paul. [33]Then the tribune came up and arrested him, and ordered him to be bound with two chains. He inquired who he was and what he had done. [34]Some in the crowd shouted one thing, some another; and as he could not learn the facts because of the uproar, he ordered him to be brought into the barracks. [35]And when he came to the steps, he was actually carried by the soldiers because of the violence of the crowd; [36]for the mob of the people followed, crying, "Away with him!"

37 As Paul was about to be brought into the barracks, he said to the tribune, "May I say something to you?" And he said, "Do you know Greek? [38]Are you not the Egyptian, then, who recently stirred up a revolt and led the four thousand men of the Assassins out into the wilderness?" [39]Paul replied, "I am a Jew, from Tarsus in Cilicia, a citizen of no mean city; I beg you, let me speak

to the people." [40]And when he had given him leave, Paul, standing on the steps, motioned with his hand to the people; and when there was a great hush, he spoke to them in the Hebrew language, saying:

third time (recall Jesus' three predictions of his own fate in Jerusalem) Paul is warned again as to what awaits him in Jerusalem. At this moment we hear again of the Philip whom we came to know briefly in the earlier stories about Samaria; we meet him here and his four daughters who enjoy the gift of prophecy. But it is a certain Agabus from Judea who, like the prophets of old who told of the impending trials of great Israelite leaders, gives the mesmerizing sign and then interprets in mystery. Paul's answer to the pleas to avoid this imminent sorrow is that of the heroic disciple: he is ready for death itself, he wants only that the Lord's will be done. We see ever more clearly the meaning of Jesus' words to Ananias about the blind Paul in Damascus: not only is he the instrument by which the Lord's name is brought to the Gentiles, but the Lord will himself indicate to Paul how much he will have to suffer "for my name." We have seen how these two mandates, witnessing and suffering, have been interwoven through Turkey and Macedonia to Greece; we now turn to Jerusalem.

Paul reaches Jerusalem and stays in the house of a Jewish Hellenist Christian; he is warmly welcomed by all and the next day makes a formal visit to the leaders of the Jerusalem Church, who are described as James (not one of the Twelve, but a brother of Jesus) and the elders or presbyters, like those we found, for example, in Ephesus. As elsewhere, so here, Paul relates the wonderful response the Gentiles have made to the name of the Lord; for this all praise God, thus indicating that the leadership of Jerusalem has an approving attitude to what Paul has done and taught, contrary to what these leaders must now report to Paul.

Interwoven throughout Acts is the difference of understanding among Christians themselves concerning this relationship between the thousand-year-old Mosaic/Abrahamic approach to God and the discipleship of Jesus. Many Palestinian Jews tried to integrate both old and new so that both become a necessity for salvation. The events of chapter 15 made clear what the policy of the Church leadership was in this regard; yet, many others of the Jerusalem Church, while agreeing on the one thing necessary for salvation— Jesus—kept up their Jewish practices. It is this group of Jewish Christians who have formed an opinion of the manner in which Paul has preached the decision of chapter 15. For them, he has not only accentuated Jesus as the one thing necessary for salvation, but he has denigrated any value of Moses, whether it be in regard to the practice, originating with Abraham, of circumcision or to the practice of other customs. They resented Paul's teaching the Gentiles that everything but Jesus is relative and unimportant.

Paul himself, of course, is a Jew, and we have noted how often he practices customs of Judaism while being a Christian; even now he has hurried to Jerusalem to be on time to celebrate the Jewish feast of Pentecost—something that many Jews outside Israel would not feel obliged to hurry to do. Given Paul's Jewish activities, the Jerusalem leadership sees a way of disproving the mumblings and complaints of Jewish Christians against Paul. As Paul had ended a period of dedication to God by following the prescriptions of the Mosaic law which asked for a shaving of one's head, would not Paul pay the cost of the head-shaving of the four Christians who were nearing the end of the time of their special vows, as well as the cost of the animal sacrifice in the temple which follows upon the head-shaving? Paul could even join these four men in the fuller temple rites associated with the completion of these vows. Such cooperation would dispel the ugly whisperings against Paul's insensitivity to Moses' law. Indeed, in part, these angry Jewish Christians had been placated as the Jewish Jerusalem leadership had asked of the Gentiles and observance of at least four prescriptions of the Mosaic law which Jews, inside and outside Israel, expect all their associates to keep.

Paul is very willing to do what is asked of him, and enters the temple area. The fateful step is taken, for it is in this temple area that Paul is seized and brought outside the temple building itself, but still within the temple area which surrounds the temple building, in order to be put to death. Why death? Because surrounding the temple building itself is a series of stones which forbid any non-Jew, under pain of death, from crossing from the temple area across this line of stones, for beyond this line of stones is the sacred area reserved for the people of Israel alone. The crowd, stirred up by Jews from around Ephesus who thought Paul despised the Jewish religion, had heard the rumor that Paul had brought a Gentile past the line of stones; the Gentile and his "supporter" deserved death.

What saved Paul was the fact that in the northwest corner of the temple area or precinct stood the fortress Antonia, a large military compound built by Herod the Great precisely so that from the fortress Roman soldiers could look down onto the temple area and spot any trouble brewing among the milling crowds there. Indeed, stairs were built from temple precinct to fortress, so that the soldiers could have immediate access to the temple area in emergencies. And Paul's case was an emergency!

The Roman soldiers, and not the temple police, separate Paul and the crowd, tying Paul in chains, then trying to get answers to what has caused all this bitterness. To get a clear answer the Roman military commander decided to take Paul up the stairs to the fortress, indeed carried him up the stairs part-way because of the violence of the crowd. It is on these stairs that Paul reveals his Roman citizenship and wins the opportunity to speak his own defense to his fellow Jews; he chooses to speak in Hebrew.

Luke has taken some time to describe in good detail
this turning point in Paul's career. The time spent on this
moment is determined in part because it is so important as
an explanation as to how Jesus' will is carried out in spe-
cifics: witness to the end of the earth, suffer for my name.
Luke also is here, as elsewhere, following the literary obli-
gation of his time, to give his readers interesting stories as
well as more summary statements, in order to entertain the
reader and not bore him with always the same kind of re-
portage. But it is also bittersweet to recall that it was in
compliance with a desire to placate his own enemies from
within Christian ranks that all this was given a chance to
come about.

22

Paul Defends Himself • He Is Saved from Scourging by His Roman Citizenship and Appears Before the Sanhedrin

Paul stands before this crowd of his fellow Jews because they think it necessary not to argue whether or not he actually brought a Gentile beyond the barriers meant to restrain Gentiles from the house of God, but to justify to Jews his many years' presence among the Gentiles of the Mediterranean. To this end Paul does two things: first, he tells of his foundational experience on the way to Damascus; second, he recounts the important circumstances of this experience in a particularly "Jewish" way, and adds to the experience a second divine intervention. Let us see this in detail.

What Luke, as narrator, told his readers in chapter 9 is now reformulated and narrated by the main actor, Paul. Essentially however, the two stories do coincide and harmonize, even to some points of identity, in particular the exchange: "Saul, Saul, why do you persecute me?" "Who are you, sir?" "I am Jesus (the Nazorean) whom you are persecuting."

Since Paul is repeating essentially what the reader already knows through Luke's trustworthy report, the reader knows that Paul is telling the truth to his fellow Jews in his defense. And if it were necessary, the reader should be more convinced than ever that Paul is truly a representative of Jesus. The essential point of Paul's narration, however, lies in this, that he wants his hearers to realize that what hap-

22 "Brethren and fathers, hear the defense which I now make before you."

2 And when they heard that he addressed them in the Hebrew language, they were the more quiet. And he said:

3 "I am a Jew, born at Tarsus in Cilicia, but brought up in this city at the feet of Gamaliel, educated according to the strict manner of the law of our fathers, being zealous for God as you all are this day. ⁴I persecuted this Way to the death, binding and delivering to prison both men and women, ⁵as the high priest and the whole council of elders bear me witness. From them I received letters to the brethren, and I journeyed to Damascus to take those also who were there and bring them in bonds to Jerusalem to be punished.

6 "As I made my journey and drew near to Damascus, about noon a great light from heaven suddenly shone about me. ⁷And I fell to the ground and heard a voice saying to me, 'Saul, Saul, why do you persecute me?' ⁸And I answered, 'Who are you, Lord?' And he said to me, 'I am Jesus of Nazareth whom you are persecuting.' ⁹Now those who were with me saw the light but did not hear the voice of the one who was speaking to me. ¹⁰And I said, 'What shall I do, Lord?' And the Lord said to me, 'Rise, and go into Damascus, and there you will be told all that is appointed for you to do.' ¹¹And when I could not see because of the brightness of that light, I was led by the hand by those who were with me, and came into Damascus.

12 "And one Ananias, a devout man according to

the law, well spoken of by all the Jews who lived there, [13]came to me, and standing by me said to me, 'Brother Saul, receive your sight.' And in that very hour I received my sight and saw him. [14]And he said, 'The God of our fathers appointed you to know his will, to see the Just One and to hear a voice from his mouth; [15]for you will be a witness for him to all men of what you have seen and heard. [16]And now why do you wait? Rise and be baptized, and wash away your sins, calling on his name.'

17 "When I had returned to Jerusalem and was praying in the temple, I fell into a trance [18]and saw him saying to me, 'Make haste and get quickly out of Jerusalem, because they will not accept your testimony about me.' [19]And I said, 'Lord, they themselves know that in every synagogue I imprisoned and beat those who believed in thee. [20]And when the blood of Stephen thy witness was shed, I also was standing by and approving, and keeping the garments of those who killed him.' [21]And he said to me, 'Depart; for I will send you far away to the Gentiles.' "

22 Up to this word they listened to him; then they lifted up their voices and said, "Away with such a fellow from the earth! For he ought not to live." [23]And as they cried out and waved their garments and threw dust into the air, [24]the tribune commanded him to be brought into the barracks, and ordered him to be examined by scourging, to find out why they shouted thus against him. [25]But when they had tied him up with the thongs, Paul said to the centurion who was standing by, "Is it lawful for you to scourge a man who is a Roman citizen, and uncondemned?" [26]When the centurion heard that, he went to the tribune and said to him, "What are you about to do? For this man is a Roman citizen." [27]So the tribune came and said to him, "Tell me, are you a Roman citizen?" And

he said, "Yes." [28]The tribune answered, "I bought this citizenship for a large sum." Paul said, "But I was born a citizen." [29]So those who were about to examine him withdrew from him instantly; and the tribune also was afraid, for he realized that Paul was a Roman citizen and that he had bound him.

30 But on the morrow, desiring to know the real reason why the Jews accused him, he unbound him, and commanded the chief priests and all the council to meet, and he brought Paul down and set him before them.

pened to him on the road to Damascus was caused by God's will and that the second vision of Jesus, which specifically told Paul to preach the saving news outside Jerusalem, was the reason Paul went to the Gentiles; none of this, in other words, was decided upon by Paul. To show his total dependence on the divine will is, then, the essential point of this second recital of Paul's experiences on the way to Damascus and in the temple of Jerusalem; if anyone is to "blame" for Paul's going to Gentiles, it is God himself and not Paul. Let his audience understand this!

Paul, then, repeats the basic Christian experience of his life. He does it, however, in a particularly attractive way for his Jewish brethren; at least he hopes this is so. Compared with the experience as Luke tells it in chapter 9, the rendition of chapter 22 is noteworthy for the following points. Paul twice is reported as speaking in Hebrew. He identifies himself as a Jew; his being born outside Israel does not deny his upbringing in Jerusalem itself, where he learned from a great Jewish teacher of his century, and his being educated in this way shows his devotion to the Jewish traditions. So did his dedication to the law and his efforts to defend God, even to persecuting the Christians to death. In fact, his journey to Damascus was with the approval of the Jewish authorities in Jerusalem, and this is certainly a sign of his devotion and trustworthiness. Indeed, who else was so dedicated to Judaism as to ride to Damascus on such a dangerous mission?

It is in this account, rather than in that of chapter 9, that Jesus identifies himself as a Nazorean, a point which reveals Jesus' Jewish identity, too. Ananias appears in Paul's recital, as he did in Luke's earlier description, but he is obviously described more fully and in terms which are meant to influence Paul's audience. Ananias is a devout servant of the Jewish law and highly praised by the Jews of Damascus;

is he therefore not an independent, reliable witness both to the fact that what is happening to Paul is God's will and to the fact that Paul's service to God is a service long ago planned by "the God of our fathers"? It was this laudable Jew of Damascus who instructed Paul to be baptized in Jesus' name, who told his brother Paul of his mission to witness to the Just One (a particularly notable Jewish title) before all mankind.

Finally, it is to be stressed that the second vision of Jesus occurs right in the temple precincts, right at the center of Judaism. The message is that Paul is to leave Jerusalem to go to the Gentiles, and the divine reason is the fact that Jerusalem will not listen to Paul's message of salvation. Paul shows his audience that he tried to change the Lord's order to leave Jerusalem, by pointing out to the Lord that the Jews would listen to him. Despite Paul's sympathy with his people, which is meant to encourage patience on God's part, he is sent to the Gentiles.

The Jewish audience cannot, for all Paul's efforts to show his unity with the will of Yahweh, abide hearing that the Gentiles are such objects of God's love and concern. Thus the speech is halted and Paul is hurried off to a form of interrogation which should uncover reasons which will explain satisfactorily to the Roman commander just what caused the Jews to react so violently to this one man.

As in Philippi, so here, Paul's claim to Roman citizenship because he was from Tarsus frees him from the whipping and interrogation he was to undergo. It should be remembered that Tarsus, a thriving commercial center and gateway from the Mediterranean Sea to the interior of Turkey, was given Roman citizenship privileges by Mark Antony and was confirmed in those privileges by Caesar Augustus. As a citizen of this city, which hosted famous philosophers and produced many famous scholars for the Roman Empire, Paul's claim to treatment which a Roman citizen deserves is better founded than that of the Roman commander who wants to whip him.

Faced with the citizenship of Rome, the commander knows that he has no right to keep Paul in custody. But, since Paul is Jewish, the commander, reluctant to let this matter simply evaporate, puts Paul before the highest Jewish authority for judgment. Once again, a Christian is faced with the Sanhedrin; we recall again Jesus' words foretelling such trials and assuring those who speak out on his behalf that he will speak someday on theirs, promising, too, that the Holy Spirit will guide their words when they must defend themselves before mighty authorities.

Paul tried to convince his fellow Jews that he acted out of obedience to the God of their fathers. How will he present his case to the Sanhedrin?

23

Paul Meets the Sanhedrin and Later Is Taken to Caesarea for Safety's Sake, Where He Will Be Heard by the Governor

Paul had tried to explain to his fellow Jews gathered in the temple area the truth, the motivation behind his efforts among the Gentiles of the Mediterranean world. Now he is to defend his work among the Gentiles before the Sanhedrin (which rules Israel, except where Roman law takes precedence) and the commander of the Roman force in Jerusalem. Paul will be asked to defend himself three more times after this.

Paul's fracas with the high priest (who is *ex-officio* president of the Sanhedrin and the single most honored person among all Jews) is meant to strike a delicate balance between two virtues. On the one hand, Paul's response to the high priest's cruelty is justified, for Paul's had indeed been a life lived with a clear conscience. On the other hand, Paul's continued reverence for Jewish customs and institutions—and now the high priest—reveals still further virtue in Paul. Luke expects Paul to be highly thought of in this confrontation; his opposition, however, is again seen as fundamentally unjust, weak and harsh.

Like Jesus and Peter before him, Paul stands before Israel's Sanhedrin. Unlike them, he takes advantage of the theological differences he knows exist between the elders and priests (who usually were Sadducean in outlook) and the scribes (who were normally Pharisaic in outlook). It is the Pharisees who believe in life after death; Paul, whose

SCRIPTURE TEXT

23 And Paul, looking intently at the council, said, "Brethren, I have lived before God in all good conscience up to this day." ²And the high priest Ananias commanded those who stood by him to strike him on the mouth. ³Then Paul said to him, "God shall strike you, you whitewashed wall! Are you sitting to judge me according to the law, and yet contrary to the law you order me to be struck?" ⁴Those who stood by said, "Would you revile God's high priest?" ⁵And Paul said, "I did not know, brethren, that he was the high priest; for it it written, 'You shall not speak evil of a ruler of your people.' "

6 But when Paul perceived that one part were Sadducees and the other Pharisees, he cried out in the council, "Brethren, I am a Pharisee, a son of Pharisees; with respect to the hope and the resurrection of the dead I am on trial." ⁷And when he had said this, a dissension arose between the Pharisees and the Sadducees; and the assembly was divided. ⁸For the Sadducees say that there is no resurrection, nor angel, nor spirit; but the Pharisees acknowledge them all. ⁹Then a great clamor arose; and some of the scribes of the Pharisees' party stood up and contended, "We find nothing wrong in this man. What if a spirit or an angel spoke to him?" ¹⁰And when the dissension became violent, the tribune, afraid that Paul would be torn in pieces by them, commanded the soldiers to go down and take him by force from among them and bring him into the barracks.

11 The following night the Lord stood by him and said, "Take courage, for as you have testified about me at Jerusalem, so you must bear witness also at Rome."

12 When it was day, the Jews made a plot and bound themselves by an oath neither to eat nor drink till they had killed Paul. [13]There were more than forty who made this conspiracy. [14]And they went to the chief priests and elders, and said, "We have strictly bound ourselves by an oath to taste no food till we have killed Paul. [15]You therefore, along with the council, give notice now to the tribune to bring him down to you, as though you were going to determine his case more exactly. And we are ready to kill him before he comes near."

16 Now the son of Paul's sister heard of their ambush; so he went and entered the barracks and told Paul. [17]And Paul called one of the centurions and said, "Take this young man to the tribune; for he has something to tell him." [18]So he took him and brought him to the tribune and said, "Paul the prisoner called me and asked me to bring this young man to you, as he has something to say to you." [19]The tribune took him by the hand, and going aside asked him privately, "What is it that you have to tell me?" [20]And he said, "The Jews have agreed to ask you to bring Paul down to the council tomorrow, as though they were going to inquire somewhat more closely about him. [21]But do not yield to them; for more than forty of their men lie in ambush for him, having bound themselves by an oath neither to eat nor drink till they have killed him; and now they are ready, waiting for the promise from you." [22]So the tribune dismissed the young man, charging him, "Tell no one that you have informed me of this."

23 Then he called two of the centurions and said, "At the third hour of the night get ready two hundred soldiers with seventy horsemen and two hundred spearmen to go as far as Caesarea. [24]Also provide mounts for

Paul to ride, and bring him safely to Felix the governor."
²⁵And he wrote a letter to this effect:

26 "Claudius Lysias to his Excellency the governor Felix, greeting. ²⁷This man was seized by the Jews, and was about to be killed by them, when I came upon them with the soldiers and rescued him, having learned that he was a Roman citizen. ²⁸And desiring to know the charge on which they accused him, I brought him down to their council. ²⁹I found that he was accused about questions of their law, but charged with nothing deserving death or imprisonment. ³⁰And when it was disclosed to me that there would be a plot against the man, I sent him to you at once, ordering his accusers also to state before you what they have against him."

31 So the soldiers, according to their instructions, took Paul and brought him by night to Antipatris. ³²And on the morrow they returned to the barracks, leaving the horsemen to go on with him. ³³When they came to Caesarea and delivered the letter to the governor, they presented Paul also before him. ³⁴On reading the letter, he asked to what province he belonged. When he learned that he was from Cilicia ³⁵he said, "I will hear you when your accusers arrive." And he commanded him to be guarded in Herod's praetorium.

preaching had as its cornerstone the resurrection of Jesus to life after death, immediately cites this belief as the central reason for his being on trial (whereas he supposedly was on trial because he presumably brought a Gentile into an area forbidden to Gentiles). By making everything turn on belief in resurrection from the dead, Paul immediately divides his audience into two parts and in such wise that they start to argue among themselves. Indeed, the Pharisees, who will not allow the resurrection from the dead to be challenged by anybody, are willing, for the sake of principle at least, to take sides with Paul against the Sadducean members of the Sanhedrin. All this ends in such an uproar that the trial is abandoned and Paul is remanded to the commander's headquarters for overnight keeping. The high priest, however, will be heard from again, in Caesarea and at the behest of the governor or prosecutor of all Israel.

Paul has borne witness to Jesus in his speech in the temple area, only to come within a hair's breadth of dying; he has more recently at least got to the point of singling out the resurrection from the dead (intending Jesus' resurrection, principally) as his belief when he again brushes up against violent death. Now, Jesus appears to Paul and offers him consolation and encouragement. Paul is to give witness here, yes, but he is destined to give witness also in Rome. He must persevere on Jesus' behalf. With this consoling vision Luke reminds his reader that the thread running through this tempestuous narrative is still that woven from Acts 1:8: my witnesses to the ends of the earth. These stories, then, become fitted into a greater purpose, a greater order; by being absorbed into this greater order, this greater purpose, these stories can contribute their utmost to assure Theophilus that the things he has been taught are reliable.

Paul faces not only an angry mob and dangerous authority; he now is the object of plotting for his very life, as was Jesus before him. The plot is foiled by good fortune; the result of it all is that the Roman commander in Jerusalem sends Paul away to Caesarea under a very heavy guard. Heavy guard indeed, for the Roman commander knows the probable fate which will await him, should he lose a Roman citizen to the plotting of non-Romans.

Luke has alerted us already to the number of Roman officials who, left to themselves, find nothing wrong with Christianity vis-à-vis Roman law or traditions; indeed, Luke makes sure that his readers hear these opinions of Rome regarding Christianity. Many scholars see in this series of judgments Luke's subtle attempt to influence contemporary and future Roman rulers as they must in their turn evaluate Christianity against Roman law.

Paul journeys under heavy guard about thirty miles to Antipatris (founded by Herod the Great and named by him for his father, Antipater). From Antipatris Paul went another thirty miles to Caesarea-by-the-sea, where the governor or procurator (a later successor of Pontius Pilate who was a procurator, too) had his ordinary residence among many pagans; though Roman ruler of Jerusalem, the procurator, like so many pagans, preferred to go to Jerusalem, among the staunch Jewish believers, only when he had to. Here will be Paul's last moments in Israel.

24

The Roman Governor Hears Paul • Paul Teaches the Governor and His Wife, But Remains in Custody for Two Years

Each of Paul's two self-defenses, in the temple and before the Sanhedrin, ended in life-threatening situations. Paul is now brought to Marcus Antonius Felix, governor or procurator of Israel, appointed by Emperor Claudius. Felix ruled from 52 to 59 A.D., and he ruled ruthlessly; he contributed a great deal to the unrest which eventually led to the war of rebellion, 66–70 A.D., and to the destruction of Jerusalem.

The high priest and some of the elders of the Sanhedrin, those of noble family and wealth, come before Felix also— and with their lawyer, Tertullus. Tertullus' speech, like that of Paul's which follows, is tinged with qualities typical of addresses before magistrates in court cases; particularly noteworthy are the introductions in these speeches and Tertullus' laying out of the accusations succinctly, leaving the examination of the accused to the governor.

The accusations are valuable, for they reinforce what we have heard from so many other New Testament sources to be the wrongs of Christianity, particularly as these wrongs might stir Roman authority to action. Paul is a troublemaker; to the Romans, this is cause enough to pursue the case, to cause anxiety. Paul encourages revolt among Jews all over the world; recall that in Thessalonica Paul was accused before Romans of preaching a king other than Caesar. Further, the Christians are identified as a sect from the north of Israel, which is particularly noted in these years for its rebellious

24 And after five days the high priest Ananias came down with some elders and a spokesman, one Tertullus. They laid before the governor their case against Paul; ²and when he was called, Tertullus began to accuse him, saying:

"Since through you we enjoy much peace, and since by your provision, most excellent Felix, reforms are introduced on behalf of this nation, ³in every way and everywhere we accept this with all gratitude. ⁴But, to detain you no further, I beg you in your kindness to hear us briefly. ⁵For we have found this man a pestilent fellow, an agitator among all the Jews throughout the world, and a ringleader of the sect of the Nazarenes. ⁶He even tried to profane the temple, but we seized him. ⁸By examining him yourself you will be able to learn from him about everything of which we accuse him."

9 The Jews also joined in the charge, affirming that all this was so.

10 And when the governor had motioned to him to speak, Paul replied:

"Realizing that for many years you have been judge over this nation, I cheerfully make my defense. ¹¹As you may ascertain, it is not more than twelve days since I went up to worship at Jerusalem; ¹²and they did not find me disputing with any one or stirring up a crowd, either in the temple or in the synagogues, or in the city. ¹³Neither can they prove to you what they now bring up against me. ¹⁴But this I admit to you, that according to the Way, which they call a sect, I worship the God of our fathers, believing everything laid down by the law or written in the prophets, [15]having a hope in God which these themselves accept, that there will be a resurrection of both the just and the unjust. [16]So I always take pains to have a clear conscience toward God and toward men. [17]Now after some years I came to bring to my nation alms and offerings. [18]As I was doing this, they found me purified in the temple, without any crowd or tumult. But some Jews from Asia— [19]they ought to be here before you and to make an accusation, if they have anything against me. [20]Or else let these men themselves say what wrongdoing they found when I stood before the council, [21]except this one thing which I cried out while standing among them, 'With respect to the resurrection of the dead I am on trial before you this day.' "

22 But Felix, having a rather accurate knowledge of the Way, put them off, saying, "When Lysias the tribune comes down, I will decide your case." [23]Then he gave orders to the centurion that he should be kept in custody but should have some liberty, and that none of his friends should be prevented from attending to his needs.

24 After some days Felix came with his wife Drusilla, who was a Jewess; and he sent for Paul and heard him speak upon faith in Christ Jesus. [25]And as he argued about justice and self-control and future judgment, Felix was alarmed and said, "Go away for the present; when I have an opportunity I will summon you." [26]At the same time he hoped that money would be given him by Paul. So he sent for him often and conversed with him. [27]But when two years had elapsed, Felix was succeeded by Porcius Festus; and desiring to do the Jews a favor, Felix left Paul in prison.

tendencies and acts of violence against Roman authority (note that though for years followers of Jesus were known as Christians, it serves Tertullus' purposes to call them here by a name which would cause Felix preoccupation). Finally, Paul is accused of something which is more horrendous to Jews than to Romans, yet would make Romans fidget because of the implications of temple desecration for public peace and order. To all these charges two or more Jews bear witness and assure Felix that these are the facts.

As was customary, the prisoner is now given his chance to respond to the charges made public against him. Though his accusers did not refer to the one incident which has led to two previous trials and now this one before Felix, Paul refers to it. Neither at that time, nor at any other time since Paul arrived in Jerusalem twelve days ago, has any of those accusers present found Paul debating or inciting people. Thus, Paul contradicts the charge of incitement to sedition and public disturbance put before Felix. That there exists a sect—Paul prefers to call it a new way of worshiping the God of Israel—is true, but it insists that it is rooted squarely in the normative documents of Judaism. By saying this, Paul means to undercut any suggestion that the Christians are a public threat to the religion of the land. Paul now introduces a particular argument meant to appeal to those who know Judaism only from the outside, but who recognize the value of virtuous living with a view to an afterlife of reward. His contention that his conscience is clear before God and man cannot be taken lightly.

Paul returns to the one "crime" he was supposed to have committed and for which he has been made a prisoner: desecration of the temple reserved for Jews only. In his brief description of the circumstances of his visit to the temple, he is seen to be quite the opposite of one who cares little for his people and the practices of Judaism; moreover, he

never encouraged a crowd around himself when in the temple area—a fact the Romans would hope to be true.

Finally, Paul points to a technical fault in the trial. His
accusers are not the correct accusers; the ones who should
be witnesses against him are not present. Those who are
present can only provide second-hand witness, and that is
not really sufficient or just. If they want to confront him
now with an accusation which the Sanhedrin and the Roman
commander in Jerusalem had considered, then Felix should
understand that that accusation had to do with Paul's belief
in the resurrection from the dead—and why should Felix
find such a belief punishable?

By now Felix has figured out what other Roman officials
before him had concluded, that this accusation and counter-
accusation has nothing to do with upsetting Roman order
or institutions, but is a squabble within a limited religion.
But Felix, for his own purposes, does not free Paul; rather
he procrastinates under the pretext of hearing the presumably unprejudiced viewpoint of the Roman commander who
was on the scene when Paul was attacked in the temple area
and heard him before the Sanhedrin in Jerusalem.

Paul is kept in Caesarea, but under loose guard; this is
a sign of his actual innocence. A further sign is the positive
interest Roman authority takes in "the Way." Felix and his
wife, Drusilla, born in 38 A.D. to Herod Agrippa I (who died
in 44 A.D., in Caesarea, after beheading James and imprison-
ing Peter), sought firsthand information about this belief in
Jesus. But the "new Way" involved more than belief alone
in Jesus; it involved uprightness—and Felix was an extremely cruel and unjust man. It also involved continence—
and both Felix and Drusilla, who were married in 54 A.D.,
were flamboyant practitioners of divorce, each eventually
being married three times. (John the Baptist would not let
Herod Antipas divorce and remarry once.) Since they were

unjust and incontinent, they would hardly be inclined to listen long to affirmations about judgment for sins. And so Paul, though called often enough before Felix, lived in a kind of prisoner's limbo. With some freedom, he still was restrained and stayed that way until Felix was finally called back to Rome on charges of injustice in his rule—Felix, it seems, hopes that Paul would eventually seek his freedom through bribery, but Paul stayed a prisoner for two years, only to meet in Festus, Felix's successor, another governor with the wrong motive for keeping Paul under arrest.

Once again, then, Christianity, put to the test, is hardly found a threat to anyone who is unprejudiced; its opponents, for all their power and cleverness, are defeated. It is the victory of God over those who would halt the witness to Jesus and to the kingdom he offers to those who believe in him.

25

In an Exchange with the New Governor Paul Asks for a Trial in Rome • The Governor Prepares the Case for Rome

Porcius Festus was appointed governor of Israel by Emperor Nero in 60 A.D., after Felix had been removed from the governor's office. Felix was apparently an upright man who tried to alleviate the growing tensions between Jews and Rome; unfortunately, he died after only two years in office, and the efforts at revolution from Rome continued to their disastrous culmination.

As a new appointee, Festus tried immediately to win over the government and people over whom he was to rule; he went to Jerusalem shortly after his arrival from Rome as a gesture of good will. There it was that leading Sanhedrinists pressed the governor to have Paul brought to Jerusalem to stand trial in the city where he had committed his crime of bringing a Gentile beyond city limits. Actually, their plan was to kill him on the way from Caesarea to Jerusalem, just as an earlier group had planned to kill Paul, once his trial before the Sanhedrin in Jerusalem had been aborted and Paul was to be taken to Caesarea. This time, the governor preferred to judge Paul in Caesarea rather than in Jerusalem, and thus he unwittingly foiled the real purpose behind the request that Paul be put on the road to Jerusalem. True to his intent, the governor prepared to try Paul in Caesarea by asking the leading men of the Sanhedrin to come with him to Caesarea for the trial. This they did.

So now the beleaguered Paul, after defenses in the tem-

25 Now when Festus had come into his province, after three days he went up to Jerusalem from Caesarea. ²And the chief priests and the principal men of the Jews informed him against Paul; and they urged him, ³asking as a favor to have the man sent to Jerusalem, planning an ambush to kill him on the way. ⁴Festus replied that Paul was being kept at Caesarea, and that he himself intended to go there shortly. ⁵"So," said he, "let the men of authority among you go down with me, and if there is anything wrong about the man, let them accuse him."

6 When he had stayed among them not more than eight or ten days, he went down to Caesarea; and the next day he took his seat on the tribunal and ordered Paul to be brought. ⁷And when he had come, the Jews who had gone down from Jerusalem stood about him, bringing against him many serious charges which they could not prove. ⁸Paul said in his defense, "Neither against the law of the Jews, nor against the temple, nor against Caesar have I offended at all." ⁹But Festus, wishing to do the Jews a favor, said to Paul, "Do you wish to go up to Jerusalem, and there be tried on these charges before me?" ¹⁰But Paul said, "I am standing before Caesar's tribunal, where I ought to be tried; to the Jews I have done no wrong, as you know very well. ¹¹If then I am a wrongdoer, and have committed anything for which I deserve to die, I do not seek to escape death; but if there is nothing in their charges against me, no one can give me up to them. I appeal to Caesar." ¹²Then Festus,

when he had conferred with his council, answered, "You have appealed to Caesar; to Caesar you shall go."

13 Now when some days had passed, Agrippa the king and Bernice arrived at Caesarea to welcome Festus. [14]And as they stayed there many days, Festus laid Paul's case before the king, saying, "There is a man left prisoner by Felix; [15]and when I was at Jerusalem, the chief priests and the elders of the Jews gave information about him, asking for sentence against him. [16]I answered them that it was not the custom of the Romans to give up any one before the accused met the accusers face to face, and had opportunity to make his defense concerning the charge laid against him. [17]When therefore they came together here, I made no delay, but on the next day took my seat on the tribunal and ordered the man to be brought in. [18]When the accusers stood up, they brought no charge in his case of such evils as I supposed; [19]but they had certain points of dispute with him about their own superstition and about one Jesus, who was dead, but whom Paul asserted to be alive. [20]Being at a loss how to investigate these questions, I asked whether he wished to go to Jerusalem and be tried there regarding them. [21]But when Paul had appealed to be kept in custody for the decision of the emperor, I commanded him to be held until I could send him to Caesar." [22]And Agrippa said to Festus, "I should like to hear the man myself." "Tomorrow," said he, "you shall hear him."

23 So on the morrow Agrippa and Bernice came with great pomp, and they entered the audience hall with the military tribunes and the prominent men of the city. Then by command of Festus Paul was brought in. [24]And Festus said, "King Agrippa and all who are present with us, you see this man about whom the whole Jewish people petitioned me, both at Jerusalem and here, shout-

ing that he ought not to live any longer. [25]But I found that he had done nothing deserving death; and as he himself appealed to the emperor, I decided to send him. [26]But I have nothing definite to write to my lord about him. Therefore I have brought him before you, and, especially before you, King Agrippa, that, after we have examined him, I may have something to write. [27]For it seems to me unreasonable, in sending a prisoner, not to indicate the charges against him."

ple area, before the Sanhedrin and commander of the Roman forces in Jerusalem, and before leaders of the Sanhedrin and the Roman governor Felix, must defend himself once again, before the Sanhedrin leaders and the Roman governor Festus in Caesarea.

This trial, occurring in 60 A.D., is told briefly by Luke, for he wants to concentrate on a second sitting of officials, which will include Herod Agrippa II—yet another detail to remind us of Jesus: Jewish accusations went unproved; Paul's contention of innocence before Judaism and Roman law could not be proved false. But Luke, though interested in spending much time in these chapters in describing the tribulations of the Christian hero for his reader's admiration and learning, never loses touch with that greater story with which he is vitally concerned. To begin things, Paul had expressed his intention, without ever realizing the implications of what he was saying, of going to Rome (Acts 19:21). Later, without precise knowledge of details, Paul reveals that the Holy Spirit has made it clear that he must suffer hardships and chains (Acts 20:23); his friends sense that they will never see Paul again (Acts 20:38). Twice more Paul is told not to go to Jerusalem (Acts 21:4.12). The Lord himself later assures Paul that, as he has given testimony to Jesus in Jerusalem, so must he do in Rome (Acts 23:11). And now, two years later, Paul stands in a court in Caesarea, apparently innocent of charges. Yet, when pressed with the suggestion that he go to Jerusalem for still further trial and knowing he would never get to Jerusalem alive, he appeals to his Roman citizenship and, in desperation, demands a trial before Caesar in Rome. And now we see clearly in what way Luke had in mind that witness to Jesus would be carried to Rome by Paul.

As one reads on about Paul's misadventures and various imprisonments, trials and hardships, one becomes increasingly aware that the entire last quarter of Acts is dedicated, not to reports (as in chapters 8 and 9, 13 and 14, 16 through 19) about the spread of the word of the Lord throughout the Mediterranean basin, but to one man's tribulations which will bring him, in the last verses of the book, to witness to Jesus in Rome. Why did Luke do things this way, rather than just chronicle the journey of the word of the Lord, through whoever was the missionary, to Rome and thus fulfill the Lord's command to be his witnesses even to the ends of the earth? Putting the question this way suggests these conclusions. First, Luke wanted to follow Paul, not someone else; Luke's presentation of Paul from the beginning shows his fascination with him. Second, Luke wants to underline the witness, like that of the Lord himself, which involves rejection, persecution, trial, imprisonment, threats of death itself; to this end, Luke has intentionally described Paul so as to remind the reader of Jesus in his first volume and thus has enhanced the witness of one's life, not just of one's word.

Paul, then, has appealed to Rome; Festus has no choice but to concur. To Rome Paul shall go—and with him witness to Jesus.

The governor Festus, newly appointed to Israel, should be paid a "state" visit by other authorities in Israel, and so Luke records the arrival in Caesarea of King Herod Agrippa II and his sister Bernice. At his father's death in 44 A.D., described at the end of Acts 12, Agrippa was thought too young by Emperor Claudius to succeed to the power; so Claudius gave the rule to Agrippa I's brother, who married Agrippa I's daughter Bernice. Bernice's husband/uncle died four years after he was empowered by Claudius, in 48 A.D.; now Claudius thought Agrippa I's son was old enough to rule and so made him king over some petty territories in the north and to the east of Israel. He is now King Herod

Agrippa II, who will rule till about 100 A.D. (he had tried
to avert the Jewish rebellion, but, once it started, he supported Rome unswervingly). His widowed sister lived with
him incestuously, which made them both like their young-
est, Drusilla, about whom we heard in the previous chapter.
Since Herod had made himself well acquainted with things
Jewish (though he preferred the life of other cultures), it is
opportune that he is now in Caesarea. He can hear this man
Paul personally and thus help the governor to prepare the
documents for Rome which will detail the charges for which
Paul is to stand trial in Rome. From Festus' own lips we learn
that "Paul was accused of crimes Festus did not anticipate"
(v 18), that Festus "did not know how to decide the case"
(v 20), that Festus "did not find that Paul had done anything
deserving of death" (v 25), and that Festus "has nothing definite or precise to write to Rome about Paul (v 26), that to
Festus "it seems silly to send Paul to Rome without indicating reasons why he should stand trial there" (v 27).

To resolve his dilemma, Festus asks the help of Agrippa
II. The king agrees to hear the prisoner, and so we go again
to trial. This, however, is the final defense Luke calls upon
Paul to deliver for the reader's sake. It is the last summing-
up of what we have come to know as the conversion/vo-
cation experience of Paul.

26

Paul Explains His Change of Life, Describes the Role Jesus Wants Him to Play, Claims His Innocence from Any Accusation • Festus and Agrippa Respond to Paul's Words and They Agree That He Is Innocent

Agrippa gives Paul permission to speak; Luke describes Paul as an orator, for he has him "extend his hand" as a classical orator would. Moreover, as before Felix, Paul begins his address by "winning over" his audience.

Paul's first inclination is to tell the story of how he, who was a persecutor of the Christians, came to be one of the most avid Christians, even to spreading the teaching of Jesus to the Gentiles. And he does begin in this direction, as he describes the intense dedication of his earliest life to Judaism as a Pharisee. But, lest he allow this story to distract Agrippa from his central argument, viz. his defense against unjust claims, Paul breaks with his narrative to place before the king what he thinks is the real reason for his being hounded and accused by certain Jewish authorities. The real reason for this trial is the difference of opinion between Paul (and the Christians) and other Jews over whether or not God has, through and in Jesus, fulfilled the promises which the twelve tribes pray day and night that they might see. In a dramatic gesture, Paul suddenly turns from Agrippa to address his accusers; why is it so hard for them to accept the resurrection of Jesus from the dead? It is his resurrection, of course, which is the nub of the problem for, if he is risen,

26 Agrippa said to Paul, "You have permission to speak for yourself." Then Paul stretched out his hand and made his defense:

2 "I think myself fortunate that it is before you, King Agrippa, I am to make my defense today against all the accusations of the Jews, ³because you are especially familiar with all customs and controversies of the Jews; therefore I beg you to listen to me patiently.

4 "My manner of life from my youth, spent from the beginning among my own nation and at Jerusalem, is known by all the Jews. ⁵They have known for a long time, if they are willing to testify, that according to the strictest party of our religion I have lived as a Pharisee. ⁶And now I stand here on trial for hope in the promise made by God to our fathers, ⁷to which our twelve tribes hope to attain, as they earnestly worship night and day. And for this hope I am accused by Jews, O king! ⁸Why is it thought incredible by any of you that God raises the dead?

9 "I myself was convinced that I ought to do many things in opposing the name of Jesus of Nazareth. ¹⁰And I did so in Jerusalem; I not only shut up many of the saints in prison, by authority from the chief priests, but when they were put to death I cast my vote against them. ¹¹And I punished them often in all the synagogues and tried to make them blaspheme; and in raging fury against them, I persecuted them even to foreign cities.

12 "Thus I journeyed to Damascus with the authority and commission of the chief priests. ¹³At midday, O king, I saw on the way a light from heaven, brighter than the sun, shining round me and those who journeyed with

me. [14]And when we had all fallen to the ground, I heard a voice saying to me in the Hebrew language, 'Saul, Saul, why do you persecute me? It hurts you to kick against the goads.' [15]And I said, 'Who are you, Lord?' And the Lord said, 'I am Jesus whom you are persecuting. [16]But rise and stand upon your feet; for I have appeared to you for this purpose, to appoint you to serve and bear witness to the things in which you have seen me and to those in which I will appear to you, [17]delivering you from the people and from the Gentiles—to whom I send you [18]to open their eyes, that they may turn from darkness to light and from the power of Satan to God, that they may receive forgiveness of sins and a place among those who are sanctified by faith in me.'

19 "Wherefore, O King Agrippa, I was not disobedient to the heavenly vision, [20]but declared first to those at Damascus, then at Jerusalem and throughout all the country of Judea, and also to the Gentiles, that they should repent and turn to God and perform deeds worthy of their repentance. [21]For this reason the Jews seized me in the temple and tried to kill me. [22]To this day I have had the help that comes from God, and so I stand here testifying both to small and great, saying nothing but what the prophets and Moses said would come to pass: [23]that the Christ must suffer, and that, by being the first to rise from the dead, he would proclaim light both to the people and to the Gentiles."

24 And as he thus made his defense, Festus said with a loud voice, "Paul, you are mad; your great learning is turning you mad." [25]But Paul said, "I am not mad, most excellent Festus, but I am speaking the sober truth. [26]For the king knows about these things, and to him I speak freely; for I am persuaded that none of these things has escaped his notice, for this was not done in a corner.

[27]King Agrippa, do you believe the prophets? I know that you believe." [28]And Agrippa said to Paul, "In a short time you think to make me a Christian!" [29]And Paul said, "Whether short or long, I would to God that not only you but also all who hear me this day might become such as I am—except for these chains."

30 Then the king rose, and the governor and Bernice and those who were sitting with them; [31]and when they had withdrawn, they said to one another, "This man is doing nothing to deserve death or imprisonment." [32]And Agrippa said to Festus, "This man could have been set free if he had not appealed to Caesar."

it means God insists that people accept Jesus, not crucify him.

Paul's turn to his accusers he knows to be rhetorical; he expects no answer, and, satisfied that he has brought out the real reason for his being on trial, continues his story of himself as a most faithful and reverent Jew. His enthusiasm for Judaism showed him that he must oppose any distortion of it, particularly a gross one like Christianity. So, he took extreme measures against the Christians, and these are detailed. All of this autobiography is meant here, as in chapter 22, to show that Paul's becoming a Christian was the most improbable event of all, that Paul, if he had his own way, would have obliterated Christianity. If, then, he did an about-face, surely the cause must have been powerful and completely from outside Paul.

On his way to Damascus, on his self-appointed holy task, Paul experiences such a vision that, as he says to Agrippa, he could not disobey it; such a vision left Paul with no choice but a total obedience and a total change of mind and heart.

We should note certain changes Luke has made in this third presentation of Paul's encounter with Jesus. First, though Paul and his companions are affected physically by light, there is no reference now to Paul's famous blindness (is the reader presumed to remember this?). Second, there is no reference to Paul's need for guidance into Damascus or to his helplessness until someone comes to assist him and interpret the meaning of the vision for him. Third, the figure of Ananias is simply and thoroughly dispensed with. Finally, it is Jesus who, within the vision itself, explains, and in the fullest detail ever, the role Paul is to play in Christianity. The entire story we have come to know from earlier accounts has been compacted to focus on the words of Jesus; at the same time, these words have been expanded to show the depth of Paul's mission and the clear authority of Jesus behind this mission. Once one understands the most important element of the experience, the purpose for which Jesus has selected Paul, then one should understand both the nature of Paul's work and the authority which commanded him to do it. In short, how could he have refused obedience to this mission?

Paul is to be a messenger and he is to be a witness; his message and the content of his witness are both what he has seen of Jesus and what he is still to be shown about him. Like a messenger, he runs the immense risk of being identified with the message—to his benefit if the message is well received, to his detriment if the message is heartily despised.

Jesus speaks as though in anticipation of just such trials as Paul has experienced and is currently undergoing; from these attempts at silencing Paul, Jesus—yes, it is Jesus—has intervened to deliver Paul. He is to go on unstopped because Jesus wants his message, his witness to go on unstopped.

Nowhere in Acts is the mission of Paul so grandly described in such an epic fashion as it is now. It is an opening of the eyes of the world. It is a turning of the world from the darkness to the light. It is a changing of the world from the rule of Satan to the rule of God; it is on a level of reality no less than this. It is the offer, through belief in Jesus, of forgiveness of sins and of a share in God's own people. Such is the profound and glorious mission to which Paul has been called; it touches upon the very essence of the world's happiness.

In obedience to this vision Paul preached both repentance of life and conversion or return to God both in Damascus and Jerusalem and among the Gentile world, urging them to actions which truly reflect repentance. For this kind of preaching, Paul insists, he was arrested in the temple area;

thus he implies that his being arrested for bringing a Gentile into a forbidden area is a pretext, a false charge, a trumped-up accusation—they really wanted to murder Paul because of his preaching what he understood the real mind of God to be, for Jew and for Gentile.

As he concludes his speech before Agrippa, Paul claims that God's help has accompanied him to this day and has made possible all the escapes and victories which we have learned about in Luke's narrative of Paul's missionary journeys. To put the matter in its final and correct perspective, Paul claims that what he has preached has not misunderstood what Moses and the prophets have said should happen: that suffering and resurrection were sure to happen to God's Messiah, and that, once the Messiah died and was the first to rise, he would bring light to Israel and to the Gentiles. It is on this note about Jesus that Paul ends the final speech of Luke's works, the Jesus who was findable in the Old Testament, whose suffering and resurrection were already outlined there, whose preaching of light to Jew and Gentile was already set down there.

To Festus Paul's understanding of reality was madness. To Agrippa, however, who knew Judaism and its expectations very well and also knew something about Christianity, Paul begins to make sense, a little too much sense for Agrippa's comfort. Agrippa is aware that what was a defense could become a plea for his own conversion, to share in the great happiness which Paul himself experiences. Agrippa leaves the hall rather than continue on with this; all leave with him.

As in other places in Acts, so here, the authorities who hear the Christian preachers admit that there is no cause for punishment, for denial of liberty. As men see it, Paul should go free. But there is a greater force at work in all this; it is an energy which is to bring Paul, as witness to Jesus, to the ends of the earth. No opposition can prevent this, and so, in unpleasant circumstances, Paul is prepared to sail to Rome.

27

The Sea Journey from Israel to Malta; Paul Is Saved from Shipwreck and, Because of Him, So Are All on Board • He Is Saved, For He Must Reach Rome

With the time at hand to describe Paul's crossing the broader part of the Mediterranean Sea, Luke drops again into the first person plural form of narrative. This accounts for the detailed knowledge Luke gives us of this perilous voyage. Paul is noted as being under guard of a centurion, Julius, who is of the Augusta cohort; Luke had already introduced us to a centurion, Cornelius, of the Ithaca cohort. The journey begins in a way which is natural to the Lucan way of describing such a movement: people are identified, ports-of-call are named, a moment of kindness on the part of the centurion is noted, weather is shown to be a reason for a choice of route. It is only after the Rome-bound passengers had been transferred from the original ship, bound only for a port near Troy, to a vessel bound for Italy that Luke concentrates on a fifteen-day period and on the landmark of Crete.

There is a prelude of bad weather which Luke begins to announce as Paul's first ship headed past Cyprus; this weather only seemed to worsen as, in the second ship, it forced Paul and his fellow travelers to detour for safe harboring in Crete. Paul, looking to the time of year (it was almost winter, the worst time for sailing), suggested a halt at Fair Havens, Crete. Luke gives us his judgment in the

27 And when it was decided that we should sail for Italy, they delivered Paul and some other prisoners to a centurion of the Augustan Cohort, named Julius. ²And embarking in a ship of Adramyttium, which was about to sail to the ports along the coast of Asia, we put to sea, accompanied by Aristarchus, a Macedonian from Thessalonica. ³The next day we put in at Sidon; and Julius treated Paul kindly, and gave him leave to go to his friends and be cared for. ⁴And putting to sea from there we sailed under the lee of Cyprus, because the winds were against us. ⁵And when we had sailed across the sea which is off Cilicia and Pamphylia, we came to Myra and Lycia. ⁶There the centurion found a ship of Alexandria sailing for Italy, and put us on board. ⁷We sailed slowly for a number of days, and arrived with difficulty off Cnidus, and as the wind did not allow us to go on, we sailed under the lee of Crete off Salmone. ⁸Coasting along it with difficulty, we came to a place called Fair Havens, near which was the city of Lasea.

9 As much time had been lost, and the voyage was already dangerous because the fast had already gone by, Paul advised them, ¹⁰saying, "Sirs, I perceive that the voyage will be with injury and much loss, not only of the cargo and the ship, but also of our lives." ¹¹But the centurion paid more attention to the captain and to the owner of the ship than to what Paul said. ¹²And because the harbor was not suitable to winter in, the majority advised to put to sea from there, on the chance that somehow they could reach Phoenix, a harbor of Crete, looking northeast and southeast, and winter there.

13 And when the south wind blew gently, supposing that they had obtained their purpose, they weighed anchor and sailed along Crete, close inshore. [14]But soon a tempestuous wind, called the northeaster, struck down from the land; [15]and when the ship was caught and could not face the wind, we gave way to it and were driven. [16]And running under the lee of a small island called Cauda, we managed with difficulty to secure the boat; [17]after hoisting it up, they took measures to undergird the ship; then, fearing that they should run on the Syrtis, they lowered the gear, and so were driven. [18]As we were violently storm-tossed, they began next day to throw the cargo overboard; [19]and the third day they cast out with their own hands the tackle of the ship. [20]And when neither sun nor stars appeared for many a day, and no small tempest lay on us, all hope of our being saved was at last abandoned.

21 As they had been long without food, Paul then came forward among them and said, "Men, you should have listened to me, and should not have set sail from Crete and incurred this injury and loss. [22]I now bid you take heart; for there will be no loss of life among you, but only of the ship. [23]For this very night there stood by me an angel of the God to whom I belong and whom I worship, [24]and he said, 'Do not be afraid, Paul; you must stand before Caesar; and lo, God has granted you all those who sail with you.' [25]So take heart, men, for I have faith in God that it will be exactly as I have been told. [26]But we shall have to run on some island."

27 When the fourteenth night had come, as we were drifting across the sea of Adria, about midnight the sailors suspected that they were nearing land. [28]So they sounded and found twenty fathoms; a little farther on they sounded again and found fifteen fathoms. [29]And

fearing that we might run on the rocks, they let out four anchors from the stern, and prayed for day to come. [30]And as the sailors were seeking to escape from the ship, and had lowered the boat into the sea, under pretense of laying out anchors from the bow, [31]Paul said to the centurion and the soldiers, "Unless these men stay in the ship, you cannot be saved." [32]Then the soldiers cut away the ropes of the boat, and let it go.

33 As day was about to dawn, Paul urged them all to take some food, saying, "Today is the fourteenth day that you have continued in suspense and without food, having taken nothing. [34]Therefore I urge you to take some food; it will give you strength, since not a hair is to perish from the head of any of you." [35]And when he had said this, he took bread, and giving thanks to God in the presence of all he broke it and began to eat. [36]Then they all were encouraged and ate some food themselves. [37](We were in all two hundred and seventy-six persons in the ship.) [38]And when they had eaten enough, they lightened the ship, throwing out the wheat into the sea.

39 Now when it was day, they did not recognize the land, but they noticed a bay with a beach, on which they planned if possible to bring the ship ashore. [40]So they cast off the anchors and left them in the sea, at the same time loosening the ropes that tied the rudders; then hoisting the foresail to the wind they made for the beach. [41]But striking a shoal they ran the vessel aground; the bow stuck and remained immovable, and the stern was broken up by the surf. [42]The soldiers' plan was to kill the prisoners, lest any should swim away and escape; [43]but the centurion, wishing to save Paul, kept them from carrying out their purpose. He ordered those who could swim to throw themselves overboard first and make for

the land, [44]and the rest on planks or on pieces of the ship. And so it was that all escaped to land.

matter: either the harbor, or we will lose ship, cargo and human lives.

This first prediction of Paul is important for two reasons. First, dramatically, it becomes the headline for the first of three parts of a three-part story; as such, it is intended to lead into the subsequent verses which show the wisdom of Paul and the error made in not following his advice. Moreover, though one certainly has the impression of being given numerous details, nautical and otherwise, the degree of detail is in very good proportion as the description of that which follows upon Paul's forecast. Second, Paul's prediction is, in part, false: there will be no loss of life. In this way, Luke made clear what should have been the fate of the passengers according to human calculation and what actually was the fate of the passengers when left to the mercy of God.

Paul's wisdom is overridden by others, particularly by a deceptive south wind which gave people a false hope that they might hurry on to Rome in safety. The "northeaster" hit the ship as it tried to skip from one port to another; it was pushed along with only a minimum of guidance possible. Eventually, overboard went the cargo, then the ship's gear. True to stories of this kind, Luke increases the emotion and anxiety: no sun to be seen by day, no stars to be seen by night, and all hope of survival abandoned. It seems as though Paul's expectation of loss of life will prove accurate.

Adrift now for a long time without food, the ship continues its blind journey westward. Within these circumstances Paul, ever the prisoner, gives his second opinion; it is a word of encouragement, assuring no loss of life, though all must undergo the trauma of shipwreck. This second forecast is at the center of the story. It underlines the human wisdom of Paul, but also corrects him where he did not foresee correctly. The sovereign will of God is the sole de-

cider of life, and it is that all will live. What governs this
decision is God's determination that nothing will stop Paul
from reaching Rome. Human beings had, through their own
machinations, tried to halt Paul, though they did not know
he "had" to go to Rome; their plots and powers were undone
by God. Now nature and men's foolishness in it threatens
to stop Paul; all this, too, is to no avail—Paul must preach
Jesus in Rome. This notion is the ruling one in this story,
but here it is buttressed by a second: that everyone else will
survive the sea journey. Why? As a favor to the man who
describes himself as belonging to God, as a servant of the
one and true God; to be associated with the man who is
close to God is to enjoy life.

Paul's second, divinely inspired forecast occurs near the
fourteenth night of being driven across the Mediterranean
Sea. Though in darkness, the crew sensed that they were
near to some kind of land. They drop anchors and pray for
daylight, but then the sailors try a subterfuge by which they
would hope to flee the ship safely without the soldiers and
other passengers. It is Paul who catches them at this and
convinces the soldiers that, without the sailing crew, the
soldiers' lives are forfeit; they force the crew to remain on
board. Again, the details of this second of three panels are
in proportion to the prophecy with which Paul had introduced the section.

It is now time for the introduction to the third panel;
we hear again the words of Paul to the travelers, words
meant to encourage further as Paul's central prediction
comes to its fullest completion. Paul recognizes the lengthy
time of suspense, trial, and anxiety and points up their circumstance of hunger and consequent weakness for the last
surge necessary for salvation. He encourages them to take
food by which they can survive, for, in a striking recollection
of the Gospel saying of Jesus (which makes one think that

this whole sea trial in some way prefigures the greater trial for the fullness of salvation), not a hair of their heads will be allowed by God to be lost. At this, Paul puts himself to leading all in a meal, reminiscent of Eucharist (though surely not so) and of that general category of meal in which charity is expressed and God is correctly thanked—even in the face of hardship and danger.

Thus is the third panel introduced, and it concludes with the complete destruction of the ship and the notice that *all* came safely to shore. Once again, there is a nice balance between prediction and a narrative of fulfillment. Within this panel, as elsewhere, there is a moment of tension as human error tries to do away with those whom God intends to save. It is futile human error, for the centurion by now knows that he can be expected to arrive with a Roman citizen in his custody. The centurion had his own reasons for saving Paul from his soldiers' imprudence, but Luke sees his action against the greater divine governance which insists that Paul must give witness to Jesus in Rome.

The story ends as Paul had predicted; it is God who has provided salvation for Paul, and for others on account of his messenger. One wonders at times why Luke spent an entire chapter on the subject of Paul's sea voyage, with its concrete details of geography, psychology, and nautical data. One cannot lay it all to the fact that writers of this kind of story in the first century A.D. had as an ideal a kind of story-telling which, by its very variety, kept the attention of the reader. To this must be added the attention Luke gives to the protection God gave to Paul as his messenger; Paul is depicted as calm and assured, because he reflects absolute confidence in the assurance given him by the God he serves. Out of an adventure on the sea Luke has deftly told a story which underlines divine care and generosity to all who associate with his servant. When one studies the story more carefully,

one sees that the author has used significant restraint in lim-
iting both the episodes of the sea passage and the details of
the damage and wreck; he has, in effect, used enough of
each to create the sense of danger and unknown future on
a black sea so that he might enhance the appreciation of
God's ultimately sure-handed control and saving intention.
In short, there is a nice balance struck between the exigen-
cies of good story-telling and revelation of the divine control
behind our lives. And, after all, we have gone over fifteen
hundred miles in only one chapter; that represents a certain
literary economy!

28

*Paul Passes Three Months on Malta, Then
Reaches Rome, Where He Is Kept Under House
Arrest • He Discusses Jesus with the Jews of
Rome and Warns Them of Callousness and Its
Effects • The Author Leaves Paul Preaching
and Teaching*

Everyone made it safely to shore, to find that this land
was the beach of the island of Malta, which lies about sixty
miles south of Sicily's closest point. Though Paul wintered
on the island, passing three months here, Luke tells us just
two vignettes. In each case, we have a miracle story—in the
first instance one that relates an apparent miracle. But added
to the miraculous in these stories are other noteworthy qualities, scholars believe.

In the first instance, Paul shakes off a snake whose fangs
clearly had penetrated his flesh; he walks away from this bite
totally unharmed. That Paul is unharmed is interpreted by
the islanders as a sign that he is a god. Luke is beyond the
point now where he might take time to have Paul explain
that he is not a god, but certainly the awe of these pagans
is meant to extend as much as possible to the reader. We
know that Paul is not a god, but we are left to conclude that
he truly was saved (again!) from a deadly circumstance. A
second observation about this event has to do with what
was just said above: Luke did not feel the need to explain
that Paul was not a god. The reason we can suggest this is
that Luke had already resolved a similar problem before pa-

SCRIPTURE TEXT

28After we had escaped, we then learned that the island was called Malta. [2]And the natives showed us unusual kindness, for they kindled a fire and welcomed us all, because it had begun to rain and was cold. [3]Paul had gathered a bundle of sticks and put them on the fire, when a viper came out because of the heat and fastened on his hand. [4]When the natives saw the creature hanging from his hand, they said to one another, "No doubt this man is a murderer. Though he has escaped from the sea, justice has not allowed him to live." [5]He, however, shook off the creature into the fire and suffered no harm. [6]They waited, expecting him to swell up or suddenly fall down dead; but when they had waited a long time and saw no misfortune come to him, they changed their minds and said that he was a god.

7 Now in the neighborhood of that place were lands belonging to the chief man of the island, named Publius, who received us and entertained us hospitably for three days. [8]It happened that the father of Publius lay sick with fever and dysentery; and Paul visited him and prayed, and putting his hands on him healed him. [9]And when this had taken place, the rest of the people on the island who had diseases also came and were cured. [10]They presented many gifts to us; and when we sailed, they put on board whatever we needed.

11 After three months we set sail in a ship which had wintered in the island, a ship of Alexandria, with the Twin Brothers as figurehead. [12]Putting in at Syracuse, we stayed there for three days. [13]And from there we made a circuit and arrived at Rhegium; and after one day a

south wind sprang up, and on the second day we came to Puteoli. ¹⁴There we found brethren, and were invited to stay with them for seven days. And so we came to Rome. ¹⁵And the brethren there, when they heard of us, came as far as the Forum of Appius and Three Taverns to meet us. On seeing them Paul thanked God and took courage. ¹⁶And when we came into Rome, Paul was allowed to stay by himself, with the soldier that guarded him.

17 After three days he called together the local leaders of the Jews; and when they had gathered, he said to them, "Brethren, though I had done nothing against the people or the customs of our fathers, yet I was delivered prisoner from Jerusalem into the hands of the Romans. ¹⁸When they had examined me, they wished to set me at liberty, because there was no reason for the death penalty in my case. ¹⁹But when the Jews objected, I was compelled to appeal to Caesar—though I had no charge to bring against my nation. ²⁰For this reason therefore I have asked to see you and speak with you, since it is because of the hope of Israel that I am bound with this chain." ²¹And they said to him, "We have received no letters from Judea about you, and none of the brethren coming here has reported or spoken any evil about you. ²²But we desire to hear from you what your views are; for with regard to this sect we know that everywhere it is spoken against."

23 When they had appointed a day for him, they came to him at his lodging in great numbers. And he expounded the matter to them from morning till evening, testifying to the kingdom of God and trying to convince them about Jesus both from the law of Moses and from the prophets. ²⁴And some were convinced by what he said, while others disbelieved. ²⁵So, as they dis-

agreed among themselves, they departed, after Paul had made one statement: "The Holy Spirit was right in saying to your fathers through Isaiah the prophet:

[26]"Go to this people, and say,
You shall indeed hear but never understand,
and you shall indeed see but never perceive.
[27]For this people's heart has grown dull,
and their ears are heavy of hearing,
and their eyes they have closed;
lest they should perceive with their eyes,
and hear with their ears,
and understand with their heart,
and turn for me to heal them.'

[28]Let it be known to you then that this salvation of God has been sent to the Gentiles; they will listen."

30 And he lived there two whole years at his own expense, and welcomed all who came to him, [31]preaching the kingdom of God and teaching about the Lord Jesus Christ quite openly and unhindered.

gans in Acts 14:8–18. Thus, we have fallen under the influence of this author who loves both to duplicate (or even
triplicate) stories and to make one story interpret another.
Finally, we have here the story of a deadly snake which
proves harmless to God's messenger. One cannot help but
think of this isolated episode as a concrete example of what
one finds, for example, as a promise of Jesus which concludes the Gospel of Mark: "They will expel demons through
use of my name, they will speak entirely new languages, they
will be able to handle serpents safely, and they will be able
to drink poison without harm, their hands upon the sick will
make the sick recover" (Mk 16:17–18). Such a Christian
summary as this is practically in its every line verifiable in
Paul's stay on the island of Malta. It becomes clear how interwoven are single stories into the patterns of Christian
attitudes and expectations.

The second story recounted by Luke has to do with
curing the father of the island's chief figure, a cure which
led to Paul's curing the other ill people on the island. Again,
we are made to think of the quotation just given from Mark's
Gospel, i.e., the line referring to the hands which make the
sick well. We are also reminded of Jesus who cured the
mother-in-law of Peter and then laid hands upon all the sick
of Capernaum to cure them (Lk 4:38–40). We have seen so
many of these reminders of Jesus and Peter that they cannot
be just by chance; they are a way of showing the inner relationships among all these people.

With winter just about ended, Paul sailed in custody of
the centurion for Italy. He reached Syracuse, the prosperous
port on Sicily's east coast; then three days later he reached
the toe of Italy's boot, the port of Rhegium. A two-day, two
hundred mile sea journey brought Paul to Puteoli which lies
just a bit north of Naples; with this sailing finished, Paul now
goes by land the one hundred and twenty remaining miles

to Rome. Over the last fifty miles Paul was escorted by members of the already existing Roman Christian community; this gesture heartened Paul greatly. Once in Rome, he had reached, in principle, those "ends of the earth" about which Jesus had talked; he rents his own lodgings, but is under continuous guard by Roman soldiers.

From before 200 B.C. there had been a Jewish community in Rome; the leaders of this community Paul invites to his rooms, since he is not free to go to them. Obviously with intent to witness to Jesus once again before his fellow Jews, Paul feels obliged to explain exactly how it is that he is in Rome as a prisoner. His few words are a summary of what we have already heard expressed over the previous chapters of Acts; it suggests to us how Luke might have summarized the events of Jesus' life as we see them incorporated into the major speeches of Acts. Paul concludes his remarks to the Jewish leading men by laying down his final claim that the only reason he is in the situation they find him in is that he insisted on proclaiming that the hope of Israel is fulfilled in Jesus; this insistent proclamation started the chain of events which brings him to Rome as a prisoner.

The Jewish leaders claim they know nothing about Paul in particular; thus they are not prejudiced in his case. They do know, however, about Christianity—at least to the extent that it is condemned throughout the Mediterranean basin; perhaps what they have learned has come to them in a statement which would say that Christians have turned against the Jewish customs, laws and temple—such accusations we have heard from Jerusalem to Greece to Caesarea.

It falls to Paul, then, in these circumstances to try again to show to Jews the reasonableness of belief in Jesus as the completion of all the hopes raised by Moses and the prophets. Some Jews did finally see clearly the relationship of Jesus to what the Scriptures had asked Israel to look for. Others,

however, could not see their way to making this connection.
For these latter, Paul can only cite the disturbing words of
an earlier prophet of Israel about the unbelieving Jews of
his own time. It is Isaiah upon whose words Paul calls to
explain the unwillingness of these Jews to believe in Jesus.
For Isaiah, his contemporaries could look and listen all day
and all night, but they would never see or hear the truth of
what they are looking at or hearing. Why not? Because they
have intentionally made their hearts "fat," i.e., unable to be
reached by God, their ears have grown heavy and they shut
their eyes to the truth. Why have they done this to themselves? Precisely so that they can ignore God, refuse to return to him, who would surely heal them if they were only
willing. Thus Paul takes over the words of Isaiah to apply
them to his own contemporaries; the fault lies, not in the
lack of perfect harmony between Jewish expectations and
Jesus, but in the unwillingness to accept the truth which
turns one to one's God. As these words complete the Acts
of the Apostles one is sure that they should be applied more
generally than just to the Jews present to Paul on this particular day. Indeed, Jesus himself suggests, by citing the
words of Isaiah, that his speaking in parables to the Jews is
due to his awareness that it is bad will that prevents his
contemporaries from seeing and hearing the truth when it
is given to them plainly (Lk 8:9–10).

As he done twice before, Paul draws a general principle
from a particular rejection of his preaching. If the Jews will
not accept Jesus, the salvation sent them by God, the Gentiles will; it seems that the very offer of this salvation results
from the rejection of it by the Jews. In this rejection is seen
the human manner in which Jesus became the light for the
Gentiles that God had always planned him to be.

Luke concludes his story with the picture of Paul still
a prisoner with his case officially unresolved, yet, by the

grace of God, free enough—and courageous enough—to witness to Jesus and announce the kingdom of God. Paul, as did Luke throughout the two volumes, insists that the kingdom of God was present on earth when Jesus was on earth, that the king long awaited is now in place at God's right hand and to some degree ruling already the kingdom of God; it is this Jesus who has fulfilled the expectations of Scripture—all that need be done is to put oneself under his rule, i.e., to turn from Satan's rule and to live as one ruled by God. All that is left is to live forever under this kingship; whenever the king comes, we will hold up our heads for our salvation is at hand.

Conclusion

The reality Luke knows is the Christianity of Theophilus and those like him. It is a Christianity in which Jesus of Nazareth is confessed as Lord who sits at God's right hand and which is the result of a witnessing to Jesus which began through the instrumentality of the Spirit of God and reached all the way across the Mediterranean, under divine protection, to Jew and Gentile alike,

That Jesus of Nazareth sits at God's right hand means to Luke a number of things. First, this sitting at God's right hand means that, according to Jewish and Christian imagery, Jesus of Nazareth is the King of the kingdom promised to Israel (a role which is to be integrated with that of God himself). In other words, Jesus is the Messiah who reigns over the kingdom of God. Second, Jesus' past life must be brought into line with the realization that he was always destined to sit at God's right hand. This means that, if he dies, he must be raised up from the dead, for he must sit at God's right hand forever. Thus, all that Jesus did and said and suffered is to be interpreted as the actions and words and being of one designated to live forever as Messiah. Third, Jesus' sitting at God's right hand is to be understood in such a way that allows for Jesus' final coming which will bring this age to a close. Given what God knew about Jesus' death at the hands of men, it becomes clear that Jesus was never intended to bring the kingdom of God in its fullness during his public life. The public life of Jesus was newly understood as the life of the Messiah, it is true, but not the life which would bring with it the change of the ages and the fulfillment of hopes, i.e., the kingdom of God. Though Jesus was Messiah, he will close this age with the fullness of the kingdom only at the time decided upon by the Father, a time certainly to come after Jesus' resurrection from the dead.

Thus, the Christian Theophilus lives in a time which anticipates having the fullness of the kingdom and which already knows how to look upon the public life of Jesus of Nazareth, his death, his resurrection and ascension. Theophilus, as has been said, knows the truth about Jesus: he was born to live forever as King (= Lord, Messiah) at the right hand of the Father, and at the right moment to rule over the fullness of the kingdom. That Jesus died is no argument against Jesus' Messiahship; his death is permitted by God, and promptly overturned by God's raising Jesus to life again. In fact, God had said many times through the Jewish Scriptures that the Messiah would die as the free choice of men, a choice respected by God—but that he would raise up the Messiah as a counter to men's evil deed, for the Messiah *must* be alive to sit at his right hand. The freedom to kill Jesus is not a freedom that will frustrate God's overall plan for Jesus.

Jesus' public life is very important, though he did not bring about the kingdom of God in it. Its importance lies in the fact that Jesus does reveal enough about himself that one can say that he is the long-awaited Messiah. True, his death and his not bringing about the fullness of the kingdom militate against belief in him as Messiah, while his power, wisdom and holiness argue in favor of it. However, Theophilus did not have to live through those Palestinian days

of Jesus, but rather lives in the light of the resurrection of
Jesus and in the witness to Jesus of the Spirit of God, and
so is in a very good position to understand why death does
not argue against belief in Jesus. Likewise, Theophilus lives
at a time by which it is understood that Jesus, already at
God's right hand, is waiting for the divinely determined moment when he will end this age and bring the full kingdom
of God into play.

Theophilus also is in a position to see how unique is
the teaching of Jesus, a teaching which is meant for all believers in Jesus—an eternal teaching, therefore. He grasps,
too, the unparalleled font of divine power which is in Jesus,
a power of such magnitude that one can hardly call Jesus
only a human being, a power which is capable of overthrow-
ing every force which dominates man's life, a power which,
once fully released, can and will remove all obstacles to the
fullest life of God's kingdom.

Theophilus can also appreciate from hindsight the holiness of Jesus and its impact as model for all relationships
with God. The intimacy between Jesus and the Father is
unique; yet, insofar as it is able to be imitated by Theophilus,
it is the most desirable intimacy with God ever seen by this
world, and Theophilus will take Jesus as his model for relating to God.

But Theophilus knows another piece of the plan of God
which was unknown or only very dimly seen by Jesus' own
contemporaries. Theophilus sees how God planned to get
around the death of the Messiah in order to bring the message from the Messiah and about the Messiah to those Jesus
did not reach while in Palestine. God said in the Jewish
Scriptures that he wanted to offer salvation from evil powers
to all people. Jesus began this offer among the chosen people. This offer of freedom from forces which would keep

one from preparing oneself from entry into God's kingdom stopped for all, Jew and Gentile alike, with Jesus' death. With his resurrection, however, the offer was resurrected; it was the same Jesus who was offering freedom, but now it was through the help of chosen disciples and it was extended to Jews and Gentiles beyond Jerusalem, even to the ends of the earth.

These disciples did not only repeat the message of Jesus that one should repent and order one's life so that one might be worthy to enter the kingdom. They insisted that Jesus was the actual King of this kingdom, that his message of repentance included commitment to himself as the King; it made no sense to reject the King of the kingdom and still expect to be prepared to enter his kingdom.

Certain things were required, however, to make sure that the Jesus to whom Theophilus is introduced is the true Jesus of Nazareth. First, whoever was to speak on behalf of Jesus must have divine guidance and divinely inspired courage; this means that such a person must be filled with God's Spirit. Second, one must be an eye-witness of what went on in Jesus' Palestinian life and be able to interpret the actions of Jesus performed by Jesus from his position at God's right hand. If the eye-witness passes from this life, another trustworthy witness must continue the true interpretation of Jesus. Later generations must have access to the Jesus of Nazareth, for God wants people to come to him only through Jesus; it is Jesus who saves, according to God's plan. This continuity of truth about Jesus is crucial to making the true Jesus a part of the religious experience of those who are far, in distance and in time, from Palestine of 28 A.D. Finally, the witness of Jesus and from Jesus should reflect the life elements of the Master: the witness must integrate courageous oral witness with the witness of suffering. The witness' contribution, then, is truth, courage and love if it means suffering; through this kind of witness would Theophilus meet the Jesus of Nazareth, his Savior and Messiah.

The strength and wisdom of the witness is the gift of the Holy Spirit. That the witnesses to Jesus did so well is a sure sign that the Spirit reserved for the final days was poured out. Salvation is through Jesus so that one can enter the kingdom, but the power of the witness is through the Spirit.

Thus, it does not matter that Theophilus was not a contemporary of Jesus, that he did not see Jesus personally. The plan of God has arranged that all may come to know the Messiah, whatever the time and place of encounter. In short, God wanted all persons to meet Jesus as Savior. It fell to Luke to describe for Theophilus the concrete working-out of that plan and to show Theophilus—and other readers, too—exactly how they fitted into their places in the plan. For this Luke wrote one work, which we call Luke-Acts.

Bibliography For Further Reading, Study, and Reflection

THE ACTS OF THE APOSTLES

Bruce, F. *Commentary on the Book of Acts.* Grand Rapids: Eerdmans, 1960.

Crowe, J. *The Acts.* Wilmington: Glazier, 1979.

Haenchen, F. *The Acts of the Apostles.* Philadelphia: Westminster, 1971.

Karris, R. *Invitation to Acts.* Garden City: Image Books, 1978.

Kurz, W. *The Acts of the Apostles.* Collegeville: Liturgical Press, 1983.

Marshall, I.H. *The Acts of the Apostles.* Grand Rapids: Eerdmans, 1980.

McBride, A. *The Gospel of the Holy Spirit.* New York: Hawthorn Books, 1975.

Smith, T.J. *Alive in the Spirit.* Winona: St. Mary's Press, 1976.

Williams, D.J. *Acts.* San Francisco: Harper and Row, 1985.

LUKE'S GOSPEL AND ACTS OF THE APOSTLES

Juel, D. *Luke-Acts: The Promise of History.* Atlanta: John Knox, 1983.

Karris, R. *What Are They Saying About Luke and Acts?* Mahwah: Paulist Press, 1979.

Kurz, W. *Following Jesus: A Disciple's Guide to Luke and Acts.* Ann Arbor: Servant Books, 1984.

Maddox, R. *The Purpose of Luke-Acts.* Edinburgh: T. & T. Clark, 1982.

O'Toole, R. *The Unity of Luke's Theology.* Wilmington: Glazier, 1984.

Van Linden, P. *The Gospel of Luke and Acts.* Wilmington: Glazier, 1986.